Physical Characteristics of the Bernese Mountain Dog

(from The Kennel Club breed standard)

Body: Compact rather than long. Height to length 9:10. Broad chest, good depth of brisket reaching at least to elbow. Well ribbed; strong loins. Firm, straight back. Rump smoothly rounded.

Tail: Bushy, reaching just below hock. Raised when alert or moving but never curled or carried over back.

Colour: Jet black, with rich reddish-brown on cheeks, over eyes, on all four legs and on chest. Slight to medium-sized symmetrical white head marking (blaze) and white chest marking (cross) are essential.

Hindquarters: Broad, strong and well muscled. Stifles well bent. Hock strong, well let down and turning neither in nor out. Dewclaws to be removed.

Size: Height:
dogs: 64–70 cms (25–27.5 ins);
bitches: 58–66 cms (23–26 ins).

Feet: Short, round and compact.

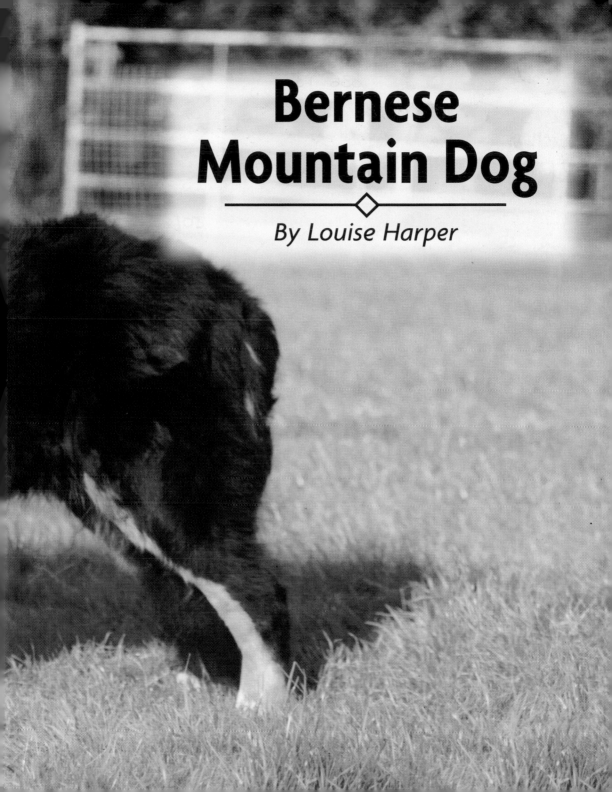

Bernese Mountain Dog

By Louise Harper

Contents

History of the Bernese Mountain Dog 9

Trace the breed's origin and development in its native Switzerland, a nation that produced four working mountain dogs. Meet the early breed pioneers credited for bringing the Bernese Mountain Dog to worldwide acclaim as well as the breeders on the Continent and in the UK who continue to work for the breed's betterment and stability.

Characteristics of the Bernese Mountain Dog 24

Find out if the Bernese Mountain Dog is the right dog for you and your family, and if you are ready for the responsiblities of owning such a special pure-bred dog. Learn about the breed's personality and owner requirements, and discover the many activities in which an owner and his active Berner can participate.

Breed Standard for the Bernese Mountain Dog . . . 30

Understanding the breed standard. Learn the requirements of a well-bred Bernese Mountain Dog by studying the description of the breed. Both show dogs and pets must possess key charac-teristics as outlined in the breed standard.

Your Puppy Bernese Mountain Dog 34

Be advised about choosing a reputable breeder and selecting a healthy, typical puppy. Understand the responsibilities of ownership, including home preparation, acclimatisation, the vet and prevention of common puppy problems.

Everyday Care of Your Bernese Mountain Dog 62

Enter into a sensible discussion of dietary and feeding consider-ations, exercise, grooming, travelling and identification of your dog. This chapter discusses Bernese Mountain Dog care for all stages of development.

Training Your Bernese Mountain Dog.............. 80

Be informed about the importance of training your Bernese Mountain Dog from the basics of house-training and understanding the development of a young dog to executing obedience commands (sit, stay, down, etc.).

Health Care of Your Bernese Mountain Dog 103

Discover how to select a proper veterinary surgeon and care for your dog at all stages of life. Topics include vaccination scheduling, skin problems, dealing with external and internal parasites and the medical and behavioural conditions common to the breed.

Your Senior Bernese Mountain Dog............. 139

Recognise the signs of an ageing dog, both behavioural and medical; implement a senior-care programme with your veterinary surgeon and become comfortable with making the final decisions and arrangements for your senior Bernese Mountain Dog.

Showing Your Bernese Mountain Dog.......... 146

Experience the dog show world, including different types of shows and the making up of a champion. Go beyond the conformation ring to working trials and agility trials, etc.

Index 156

PUBLISHED IN THE UNITED KINGDOM BY:

INTERPET
PUBLISHING

Vincent Lane, Dorking Surrey RH4 3YX England

ISBN 1-903098-78-5

PHOTO CREDITS:
Photos by Carol Ann Johnson and Michael Trafford with additional photos by
Norvia Behling, TJ Calhoun,
Carolina Biological Society, Doskocil,
Isabelle Français, James Hayden-Yoav, James R Hayden,
RBP, Bill Jonas, Dwight R Kuhn, Dr Dennis Kunkel,
Mikki Pet Products, Phototake, Jean Claude Revy,
Alice Roche and Dr Andrew Spielman

Bernese Mountain Dogs share their eye-catching Swiss tri-coloration, complemented by wonderful personalities and great physical strength. Although originally bred for working purposes, most Bernese Mountain Dogs today serve as pets to adoring owners.

ORIGIN AND DEVELOPMENT OF THE BREED IN SWITZERLAND

To discover the origins of the Bernese Mountain Dog, one must travel centuries back in time and search the mountains and the remote valleys of the Swiss hinterlands where the breed originated. Forebears of this popular Swiss dog lived and worked among the Celtic farmers of those early times, protecting both humans and livestock from natural predators.

Early history tells us that, around 1000 AD, Swiss settlers had carved out a peaceful existence on the mountainsides, co-existing harmoniously with Nature and her beasts. History also reveals that the more prosperous families kept large Swiss working dogs as protectors of the field and home. The poorer farmers, unable to feed larger animals with prodigious appetites, kept smaller dogs in keeping with their meagre budgets.

Supporting that theory, writer Conrad Gessner wrote in 1523:

'Some of the big and strong dogs are especially trained to stay around the houses and stables in the fields. They must protect the cattle from danger. Some guard the cattle, some the fields and some the houses. Other dogs are trained to protect people. They must contend after murderers and other mean people. They must be fierce and big and strong, as they must fight against warriors in their armour.'

It is apparent that their dogs were bred to perform specific tasks, although selective breeding was not yet common among the people of that time. For many generations, herding cattle was the most important duty of every mountain dog. Additionally, the dogs were used as guard dogs to give warning at the approach of wild animals, such as bears and wolves, as well as predatory humans who came to steal at any price. Although few modern dogs show evidence of these ancient instincts, many specimens of mountain dog still retain those herding and guarding instincts in their blood.

Views of Berne, Switzerland, for which the Bernese
Mountain Dog is named. Berne is the capital city of
Switzerland. It was named after the wild bears that lived
in the area. Berne was founded in 1191 and is considered
to be one of the landmark cities of the world.

In those days, the measure of any dog that was kept purely as working household inventory was in its ability and usefulness as a herder and as a protector of people and property. Conventional companion dogs were considered a useless luxury, as they were merely extra mouths to feed.

In about 1850, the mountain dogs took on another task as a working group. Local Swiss farmers, long known for making superior cheeses, built cheese plants, called cheeseries, and many used their dogs to pull carts loaded with milk cans to supply their businesses.

Prior to that time, the breed had no formal name. They were simply known as farm dogs, butchers' dogs or cheesery dogs. Understandably, they became known by their specific markings—those with white rings around their necks were not surprisingly called 'Ringgi,' dogs with distinct blazes down their face were known as 'Blassi' and those with little white markings on their faces were known as 'Bari,' which means 'little bear.' The Bari were also known as the 'Gelbackler', a name denoting 'yellow cheeks,' and those dogs with tan markings over their eyes were called 'Vieraugli,' a name which means 'four eyes.'

Given the expedient nature of the mountain dogs, the demand

GENUS *CANIS*
Dogs and wolves are members of the genus *Canis*. Wolves are known scientifically as *Canis lupus* while dogs are known as *Canis domesticus*. Dogs and wolves are known to interbreed. The term *canine* derives from the Latin derived word *Canis*. The term *dog* has no scientific basis but has been used for thousands of years. The origin of the word 'dog' has never been authoritatively ascertained.

for them was great. They were widely bought and sold, and, in the mid-1800s, the centre of such trade found itself at the Durrbachler Gasthaus. Not coincidentally, the breed soon became known as the Durrbachler, so named after that central trading post.

Around the same time, the St. Bernard's popularity was rising, thus diminishing interest in the mountain breeds. The massive St. Bernard, with his uniform coloration, captivated the dog fancy, and the tri-coloured Swiss mountain dog remained steadfast only in those remote areas where farmers and craftsmen required the use of the dogs to obtain sustenance.

In 1883 the Swiss Kennel Club was formed. Their first dog show offered a class for the St. Bernard as well as other Swiss hounds, but did not recognise the mountain dogs. Interest in the St. Bernard continued to grow, with correspondingly less attention paid to the lowly mountain dogs.

A major change in attitude occurred in 1892, when Franz Schertenleib, an innkeeper from Burgdorf, regenerated interest in the old-fashioned type of farmer's dog. Inspired by his father's tales of the breed, he embarked on a mission to preserve the dogs for future generations. Schertenleib scoured Berne for suitable breed candidates, and his quest soon sparked greater interest among proponents of other similar breeds of dog.

Most certainly the greatest

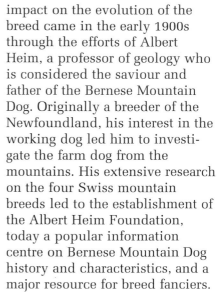

impact on the evolution of the breed came in the early 1900s through the efforts of Albert Heim, a professor of geology who is considered the saviour and father of the Bernese Mountain Dog. Originally a breeder of the Newfoundland, his interest in the working dog led him to investigate the farm dog from the mountains. His extensive research on the four Swiss mountain breeds led to the establishment of the Albert Heim Foundation, today a popular information centre on Bernese Mountain Dog history and characteristics, and a major resource for breed fanciers.

In 1904 several breed fanciers convinced the Swiss Kennel Club to open a class for the Durrbachler at a show to be held at Berne. Six dogs and one bitch were shown, and the course of the breed was set when four of those dogs were registered with the Club the following year. During the next ten years, Durrbachlers of unknown parentage were granted entry in the Swiss Stud Book, with each entry requiring the approval of one of three recognised experts on the breed: the innkeeper Franz Schertenleib; another experienced breeder, Gottlfried Mumenthaler; and a veterinary surgeon from Langnethal, Dr Scheidegger.

These three fanciers, joined by the illustrious Albert Heim, formed the first breed organisa-

ANCIENT ANCESTORS

Twentieth-century excavations in the Swiss mountain area have uncovered the skeletal remains of large dogs dating from the Bronze and Iron Ages. These dogs are assumed to be direct ancestors of today's Swiss mountain dogs. Those discoveries also bring into question another older theory that suggests that, many generations earlier, these same dogs may have been bred to the ancient Mollossus dogs of Roman times.

SWISS COUSINS

According to the FCI, there are four recognised breeds of Swiss mountain dogs: the Bernese Mountain Dog, the Greater Swiss Mountain Dog, the Appenzeller and the Entlebucher. The Kennel Club, like the American Kennel Club, only recognises the Berner and the Greater Swiss. The breeds differ mainly in size, coat length and type, all sharing the renowned Swiss tri-colour pattern.

The smallest of the quartet is the Entlebucher, who stands under 20 inches and weighs between 55 and 66 pounds. The Entlebucher is the only bobtail member of the family. The Appenzeller stands 19 to 23 inches high and weighs between 49 and 55 pounds. The giant of the quartet is the Greater Swiss or 'Swissy,' whose ancestry is likely the most ancient and is linked to the St. Bernard. The Swissy is called the Grosser Schweizer Sennenhund at home. The Swissy stands as tall as 23.5 to 28.5 inches and weighs around 130 pounds. All three breeds are smooth coated, unlike the Bernese.

The Entlebucher.

The Appenzeller.

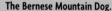
The Bernese Mountain Dog.

The Greater Swiss Mountain Dog.

tion, calling it the Schweiz-erischer Durrbach Klub. As a founding member, Heim suggested that all of the tri-colour Durrbach dogs fall under the same designation and he persuaded the club members to name the breed the Berner Sennenhund, honouring the town in which the breed had proliferated. The name was actually inappropriate to the origin and duty of the dog, as the literal translation means 'Bernese alpine (mountain) herdsman's dog,' and the Durrbach dogs came from the lowlands. However, the club, after some disagreement, approved the name change. Pursuant to that, the club also became known as the Berner Sennenhund Klub.

By the year 1908, interest in the Bernese had increased significantly, and that year the show at Langenthal sported a total of 21 entries. Two years later, in 1910, there were 42 dogs at a show in Berne. Entries continued to climb, and on 24 April 1910, the club show in Burgdorf made breed history with a record-setting entry of 107 Berners.

Professor Heim was the esteemed judge at that Burgdorf show. Many of the entries he inspected had colour variations that were no longer desirable in the breed, as well as coats that were untypical of a true breed representative. Heim was kind but honest in his criticism and

> ### DID YOU KNOW?
> In the remote farming areas of Switzer-land, the natives believed that Bernese with black feet and double dewclaws had supernatural powers to ward off evil spirits.

disqualified several dogs on the basis of their coats and markings. He also counselled the exhibitors about producing better quality animals that would contribute to the betterment of the breed.

Because Heim was held in such high regard within the breeding community, his words and the standards he set had great impact on the breeders, convincing them to improve on appearance and temperament and to eliminate poor specimens from their breeding programmes. Although some differences in colour and markings still continued, the show produced many good specimens who were ultimately admitted to the Stud Book. Breeders took note, which ultimately enhanced their breeding programmes in their quest for a more uniform-type dog.

Those efforts also served to define the Berner's characteristics as distinct from the three other Alpine breeds: the Greater Swiss Mountain Dog, the Appenzeller and the Entlebucher, with the Greater Swiss (or 'Swissy') sharing

Berners have been employed as draught dogs and cart pullers for generations. In an exhibition in Britain, this Berner is celebrating his heritage by pulling a ceremonial cart.

BRAIN AND BRAWN

Since dogs have been inbred for centuries, their physical and mental characteristics are constantly being changed to suit man's desires for hunting, retrieving, scenting, guarding and warming their masters' laps. During the past 150 years, dogs have been judged according to physical characteristics as well as functional abilities. Few breeds can boast a genuine balance between physique, working ability and temperament.

a common past with the St. Bernard. While all four breeds are 'workaholic' dogs with native herding instincts, there are major differences in type, size and coat. And while all four share the same placid, friendly disposition, there are still subtle differences in temperament. The Bernese and the Swissy, the larger of the four breeds, are today by far the better known of the Alpine breeds, and they remain more available than the smaller Appenzeller and the Entlebucher.

Throughout the first decade of the 20th century, the Bernese trailed the Appenzeller and the St. Bernard in popularity. Gradually, however, the breed became more uniform as more farmers and breeders continued to show their dogs. Breed club membership climbed to 40 members, with greater numbers of good dogs being shown on the bench. By 1917 the Berner had gained considerable ground and finally surpassed the Appenzeller in registrations; 20 years later, breed registrations also exceeded those of the St. Bernard.

Breeding practice throughout the early 1900s was sketchy at best, with many dogs of unknown ancestry used for breeding. However, by 1940 one could find pedigrees with five generations recorded, with little inbreeding in the background. But despite efforts to retain only the best qualities of the breed, correct temperament was still a problem, and club members agreed it might be necessary to introduce another breed into the gene pool.

About that time, Nature intervened and provided a solution. A Bernese bitch named Christine v Lux became pregnant when a Newfoundland dog named Pluto v Erlengut jumped the fence and accidentally mated with her. She whelped seven pups—three bitches and four dogs—on 21 December 1948, and it was no small surprise that all the puppies looked like Newfoundlands. Speculation was rampant about whether this breeding was truly accidental or was in fact a deliberate experiment to inject new blood into the Bernese breed.

Of the seven pups, one pup was retained for breeding. This was a bitch named Babette, who was given to club member Dr Hauser for future use. Babette matured with the typical temperament and conformation of a Newfoundland. When she turned three years of age, she was bred with a Berner named Aldo v Tieffurt, a breeding that produced six live and two stillborn pups. Four of the pups were incorrectly marked, with only one male and one female carrying Bernese markings. The bitch was named Christine v Schwarzwasssserbachli and was given to Herr Mischler, the president of the breed club at the time.

Mischler bred Christine at nine months of age to a Bernese named Osi v Allenluften, who was a proven producer. The pairing produced five pups, with only one male and one female surviving. The male, Alex, grew into a superb representative of the breed and won numerous awards on the bench, becoming an International Champion as well as the World Champion in 1956.

It was no surprise, then, that many Bernese breeders came to

Alex for stud service. Throughout his lifetime, he was bred to a wide variety of bitches, producing 51 litters and imprinting his offspring with many desirable Bernese characteristics. Over time, many breeders developed line-breeding programmes to capitalise on the fine qualities that were produced in the Alex matings.

THE BERNER IN ITS HOMELAND

Entering the 21st century, the Bernese Mountain Dog remains one of the most popular breeds in Switzerland, and the Schweiz-erischer Klub is one of the largest breed clubs in the country. The club maintains strict control over breeding practices through a series of assessments, called 'Ankrung,' which are held several times a year throughout the country. Officials of the breed club act as assessors to judge breeding candidates for tempera-ment and conformity to the breed standard, and only those dogs who are considered worthy specimens of the breed are passed as fit for breeding.

Hip status is also an important criterion for breeding. Because hip dysplasia is a serious genetic problem in the breed, only dogs with grades of 0 or 1 are passed as suitable for breeding. The Swiss Kennel Club also will not issue a pedigree to the offspring of any dog who is considered a poor

DID YOU KNOW?

In France and in the French part of Switzerland, the Bernese Mountain Dog is called the *Bouvier Bernois.*

specimen of the breed.

The Swiss Kennel Club maintains rigid control over the breeding community, and permits breeders to produce only one litter from any bitch in any single year, with only six puppies allowed to survive from each litter. Throughout all of Switzer-land, whenever a litter is born, the breeder must inform the area puppy controller, called a 'Wurfkontrolle.' An experienced breeder who is also a member of the breed club is assigned to oversee each area's breeding programmes. If more than six pups are born, the litter must be culled.

The reasons for culling are in the best interest of the breed. The Swiss feel strongly that only the very best specimens of any breed should be kept and bred, which charges the breeder with carefully selecting which puppies should be culled. There is also natural concern for the health of the dam and general agreement that rearing six pups places minimal stress on a nursing mother. Commendably, the breed club also worries about overpopulation and the risks of puppy mills and other irrespon-sible breeders that are an unfortunate by-product of popularity. Few breeders in Switzerland oppose these sentiments; most willingly subscribe to these breeding limitations.

The Wurfkontrolle also assist novice breeders in culling their pups as well as in other breeding issues. The culling process results in selection for correct size and markings, and the Swiss believe that will help to ensure the future quality of the breed. Pups cannot be sold until they are least eight weeks old.

The Bernese Mountain Dog is greatly revered and protected in its native Switzerland. The breed club is intensely committed to preserving the working ability of the Bernese. In fact, the entire dog community is committed to ensuring the future of the breed. Training clubs abound and many of these regularly conduct working tests. Swiss veterinary surgeons go to great lengths to educate breeders and owners about health issues. The breed club publish bulletins to keep the Bernese Mountain Dog community informed on breed issues and activities. Breed popularity elsewhere in the world

The Berner is still extremely popular in its native Switzerland, where breeders work diligently to produce outstanding bitches and dogs for their breeding programmes.

has only intensified the Swiss determination to breed the best Berners possible.

Swiss breeders have worked consistently to produce outstanding dogs and bitches in their breeding programmes. The use of Alex v Angstorf had a profound effect on the success enjoyed by many kennels. The Frau Tschanz is a sterling example of Alex's influence. Under her Dursrutti prefix, she has produced many generations of champions through a carefully constructed long-range breeding programme that incorporated Alex's bloodlines.

Amadeus Krauchi is another successful Swiss breeder who is famous throughout the US and Great Britain for his von Nesselacker Bernese dogs. Superior specimens of the breed, they won at many shows and produced equally well through the late 20th century.

We saw another world class winner in the famous Asso v Hogerbuur, who for many years was housed at the von Grunen-matt kennels, founded by Ernst Schlucter. Asso's show-ring charisma was legendary—he always thrilled both judges and spectators. He continued his legacy of excellence as a working dog in the field. Another Grunen-matt Berner, named Xodi, went to Canada to become one of the foundation Bernese in that

country. Schlucter also sent Fox v Grunenmatt to Great Britain to improve and sustain their breeding stock.

Another Bernese legend, Herr Iseli, who was a well-known breed authority and judge held in high regard, founded his von Sumiswald kennel in 1923. That kennel continued through Iseli's son, who presided as President of the Swiss breed club from 1971 to 1980. Iseli also exported his three-year-old Senta v Sumiswald to England in 1936. Co-owned by Mrs Perry and Mrs Patterson, Senta was the first Bernese to be imported to Great Britain.

THE BERNESE MOUNTAIN DOG IN GREAT BRITAIN

Mrs Perry of the Kobe kennels and Mrs Patterson of the Fontana kennels were Samoyed breeders who decided to establish the Bernese in their native England. After acquiring Senta, the first Bernese to be imported into England, their next breed acquisi-tions arrived the following year, all under two years of age. These were a male named Quell, a bitch named Nelly and an in-whelp bitch named Laura, all bred by Fritz Stalder of the Haslebacher kennel; another male, Dani, bred by Herr Haslebacher; and a third bitch, Cacilie, who was bred by Herr Schmid. Laura whelped four pups while still in quarantine in 1937; the pups were named Alex,

Bruno, Nero and Berna. These pups were the first Bernese to be born in Great Britain, and they went on to establish more of the foundation of the breed in that country. Mrs Perry bred Dani and Nelly the following year, thus helping to establish other Bernese breeding kennels.

The Second World War interrupted Bernese breeding programmes. Just as with many other breeds of dog, the few Bernese pups and adults then on the island were given away to homes who could afford to feed and care for them, and the breed literally disappeared during that time.

The Bernese remained virtually nonexistent until about two decades later, when Mrs Irene Creigh, a breeder of Mastiffs, discovered a charming-looking dog called the Bernese Mountain Dog in a photograph sent to her by a Mastiff client in Switzerland. Mrs Creigh collaborated with her friend, Mrs Mabel Coates, and the two women imported two Bernese: a male pup from Herr Mathez and a young bitch from Herr Kobel.

While these two imports were still in quarantine, a rabies alert created a freeze on quarantined dogs and none was permitted to leave after the normal quarantine period had expired. Mrs Coates arranged for the two dogs to be mated during their prolonged confinement. They were born

under Mrs Coates's Nappa kennel affix. Three of the pups went to serious breeders and went on to become foundation dogs for three successful Bernese kennels.

One of the three, Black Magic of Nappa, was purchased and campaigned by Joyce Collis. Although never widely used at stud, 'Berni' became a high-profile representative for the Bernese when he appeared on a popular children's television programme, *Magpie*. Berni was later shipped to Mr Dick Schneider in the United States, where he won Best of Breed at his first show in that country. His career was unfortunately short-lived, however, when he died of heat stroke the following year.

Meanwhile, it was Mrs Creigh who had the greater impact on the Berner's proliferation in Great Britain. She continued to expand her breeding programme, using the two original imports, Dora and Oro, as the foundation for her stock. Her dedication was responsible for the founding of the Bernese Mountain Dog Club of England, which was later renamed the Bernese Mountain Dog Club of Great Britain. She served as secretary to the club and also started a breed newsletter while in that office.

The Bernese breed club was launched in 1971 with 25 members. They held their first Open Show eight years later in 1979, to which they invited Herr

The Berner is agile and fast. It is still used for herding in Switzerland and exhibits fair endurance for its large size.

Krauchi and Herr Iseli from Switzerland to assess the dogs that were being shown. Again Mrs Creigh's contribution to the breed was evident, when both Best in Show and Best Bitch in Assessment were taken by Ch Kisumu Bonne Esperance of Millwire, a bitch she had bred and sold to Carol Lilliman. The success of holding an assessment at the show prompted the club to do so every four years, so this event was repeated at shows in 1983 and in 1987. Today the national breed club boasts over 700 members and holds two Open Shows and a Championship Show, supple-menting those events with additional assessments, working-dog events and educational seminars.

From the 1980s came the Bernese Breeders Association of Great Britain, a group of breeders and fanciers who set about to educate and distribute information on the breed. The club also sponsors

> **DID YOU KNOW?**
> In 1980, a Bernese Mountain Dog from Great Britain named Ch Folkdance at Forgeman was the first of his breed to ever win the Working Dog Group at the Crufts Dog Show.

educational seminars throughout the country and publishes a popular club magazine called *Oasis*. The club's dedication to the betterment of the breed has made great strides in the continued interest and improvement of the Bernese Mountain Dog in Great Britain.

During the last decade of the 1900s, several Bernese clubs were formed to cater to Berner owners and enthusiasts in specific regions of Great Britain: the Scottish Bernese Mountain Dog Club, the Northern Bernese Mountain Dog Club and the Southern Bernese Mountain Dog Club, which serves fanciers from the midlands to the southern coast.

THE BERNESE MOUNTAIN DOG IN THE UNITED STATES

Although there is documentation of two Bernese having been imported to America in 1926, it would be another ten years before the breed was accepted and recognised in that country. In 1935 Mr Shadow of Louisiana read an article on the Bernese written by Swiss breeder Mrs Egg Leach for the American Kennel *Gazette*. Mr Shadow had become enchanted with the breed during his youth, and he contacted Mrs Leach, subsequently arranging the importation of a male, Quell v Tiergarten, and a female, Friday v Haslenbach, the following year. These two dogs became the first imports of the breed to be recognised by the American Kennel Club (AKC) when the registry accepted the breed in 1937. The Bernese Mountain Dog and the Greater Swiss Mountain Dog are the only two Swiss mountain breeds that are recognised by the American Kennel Club.

Mr Shadow was steadfast in his commitment to his Bernese and unswerving in his efforts to promote the breed in the United States. Those efforts were thwarted by the Second World War, however, and for the next ten years Mr Shadow's dogs were the only Bernese to be registered with the AKC.

During the next two decades, breed growth was slow. The vast geography of breed enthusiasts interfered with propagating the Bernese in many parts of the country. But, by the late 1960s, there was enough interest to warrant the formation of a breed club. The Bernese Mountain Dog Club of America was launched in 1968 with just eight members. Within that first year, membership grew to 33, a newsletter was published and the club held its first 'fun' match. To their credit, the club has established a Working Dog award and a Working Dog Excellent award to honour those dogs who prove to possess the working ability of the breed. The breed has enjoyed a modest but steady rise in popularity, and during the 1990s breed registration with the AKC grew to over 2000 annually.

The Bernese
Mountain Dog
makes a
confident and
attractive show
dog. More and
more Berners are
appearing in dog
shows, proving
that the breed's
popularity is
ever increasing.

IS THE BERNESE FOR YOU?
The Bernese is a striking, tri-coloured dog, large in size, with a most amiable disposition. He is intelligent and strong, with the natural agility to perform the draught and droving work for which he was originally bred and used in his native Switzerland. He is a self-confident and good-natured dog, calm and alert, and, while he may appear aloof to strangers, he is steadfast, loyal and affectionate within his family unit. He does best as a house dog, as he is blest with a low activity level when indoors and a strong need to be near his family. He is happiest just being near his loved ones.

Given that propensity, the Bernese makes a poor kennel dog and will not thrive, indeed will be most unhappy, without human companionship. If left untended or unsupervised, he will be bored and become troublesome when not assigned a specific chore. A

Even though the Berner has, historically, been a working dog, it does brilliantly as a house dog. It still requires exercise and mental stimulation to stay in prime condition.

large garden is not sufficient in and of itself. The adult mountain dog needs long daily walks, at least an hour in length, to keep mentally and physically fit, although the Bernese under one year of age should have limited exercise to prevent damage to his immature skeletal structure.

Although the guarding ability is greatly diminished in the modern Bernese, he shows excellent judgement and will make every effort to guard and protect his human family. He also makes a good watchdog and will warn at the approach of a stranger or intruder. The possessive Berner will bark at anyone who invades his territory and hold them at bay, but only extreme action would provoke the dog into real aggression. He is considered totally reliable as a house pet and family companion.

The Bernese's herding instincts colour everything he does. A mountain dog will herd everyone and guard anything. Although he adores children, his size and playful exuberance could easily overwhelm a small child. And despite his gentle nature, he can become unruly without proper training.

The Bernese has a strong desire, indeed an indefatigable need, to work, and thus is constantly looking for a challenge or a job to do. Adaptable to many tasks, they are biddable, willing

KEEPING YOUR BERNER BURNING

Owners need to keep this active pure-bred busy and feeling productive. Here's a list of some possibilities for dog and owner:

- backpacking and hiking
- carting and draught-dog events
- obedience competition
- agility trials or working trials and tests
- dog shows
- camping
- search and rescue
- PAT dog, visiting hospitals and homes

and eager to please. They will never challenge an owner's authority if they are properly schooled at an early age.

Berners also possess a great sense of humour and often display clownish behaviour in order to be the centre of attention. They can, however, sometimes have a stubborn streak, which may lead them to be somewhat manipulative.

Surely the greatest disadvantage to owning a Bernese Mountain Dog is his brief life expectancy. Most live only seven to eight years, with a fortunate few surviving up to ten years of age.

ACTIVITIES FOR THE BERNESE MOUNTAIN DOG

There is no doubt that a Bernese is happiest when he has a job or when he is performing a task with or for his master. In their native Switzerland, as well as other countries throughout the world, many Bernese still thrive as working farm dogs—pulling carts, tending livestock and guarding their property and human families.

Berners in Switzerland also serve as rescue dogs, especially in the mountainous areas of the country, where they are specially trained for disaster work in avalanche and earthquake

Bernese Mountain Dog puppies are receptive to children and welcome their attention. This pup is enjoying a rest on a cart with his young friend.

> ## DO YOU WANT TO LIVE LONGER?
>
> If you like to volunteer, it is wonderful if you can take your dog to a nursing home once a week for several hours. The elder community loves to have a dog to visit with and often your dog will bring a bit of companionship to someone who is lonely or somewhat detached from the world. You will be not only bringing happiness to someone else but also keeping your dog busy—and we haven't even mentioned the fact that it has been discovered that volunteering helps to increase your own longevity!

emergencies. Some also work as ambulance dogs, locating injured people in crowds or wooded areas. The Bernese loves to follow scents, and so he is particularly well suited for tracking lost people. In addition to the public-service element of rescue work, Bernese now participate in rescue trials, where they can display their talents as proficient search and rescue teams.

In most countries, however, working trials offer the best opportunity for the Bernese to enjoy his heritage. Kennel clubs and breed clubs host a variety of enjoyable events to test and challenge the skills of many breeds of working dog.

Currently the sport of agility has become a top interest of the dog fancy; it is especially popular with owners of working and/or athletic dogs. Agility trials set up timed obstacle courses, each one designed for different-sized dogs. Contestants must navigate over, under, through and around tunnels, jumps, bridges and other obstacles. All breeds of dog are eligible to participate, although larger breeds such as the Bernese should not attempt jumping during their first year or two of growth, when their bone structure is still forming and quite vulnerable. The Kennel Club forbids training any dog for agility trials before the age of one year.

Carting is still the special passion of the Bernese, so it is no surprise that this activity is extremely popular with the dog as well as its like-minded owner. Both Switzerland and Sweden conduct draught-dog trials, with special courses designed specifically for them. The dogs' appetite for draught work is so strong that owners have difficulty controlling their dogs' impatience and enthusiasm during the harnessing and at the starting line. The harnesses and carts are a major part of the carting spectacle, with beautiful handwork on the harnesses and elaborate decorations on the carts.

Breed and kennel clubs in other countries also host working trials to enable the carting breeds to utilise their talents in a

DOGS, DOGS, GOOD FOR YOUR HEART!

People usually purchase dogs for companionship, but studies show that dogs can help to improve their owners' health and level of activity, as well as lower a human's risk of coronary heart disease. Without even realising it, when a person puts time into exercising, grooming and feeding a dog, he also puts more time into his own personal health care. Dog owners establish a more routine schedule for their dogs to follow, which can have positive effects on a human's health. Dogs also teach us patience, offer unconditional love and provide the joy of having a furry friend to pet!

Pulling a cart is a natural task for the Berner. For owners interested in training their Berners for draught work, there are clubs that promote trials and special meets for owners and their dogs.

productive, and often competitive, venue. As a leisure activity just for fun, most Berners in Switzerland and Germany have been shown in working harness at parades, club events and other public outings.

Showing your Bernese Mountain Dog in conformation can be an enjoyable and fulfilling activity for both dog and owner. However, there is more to this sport than merely trotting about the show ring with your dog. Whether you are a hobbyist or fierce competitor, your dog's

physical attributes and breed-specific qualities, temperament and attitude, coat condition and grooming techniques, gait and movement, as well as handler expertise, all contribute to your success in the dog-show game. If you are serious about competing in the show ring, you should first consult with your breeder or another experienced Bernese owner. It is also wise to acquaint yourself with other show fanciers to learn and understand the rules and finer points of this highly competitive canine activity.

Dog shows in Great Britain are held according to the rules and licensing regulations established by The Kennel Club. In addition to the Championship Shows, where dogs can earn the Challenge Certificates necessary to become a Show Champion, several types of show events are frequently hosted by the various canine clubs to help exhibitors gain experience and acclimate their dogs to the environment of the show ring.

OWNING A BERNESE MOUNTAIN DOG

Despite his loveable appearance and disposition, the Bernese is not the ideal dog for everyone. Potential owners would be wise to ask themselves these important questions before adding a Bernese to their family.

1. Consider your lifestyle: would a Bernese enjoy or thrive if included in your daily schedule? Do you have time to raise a puppy properly?

2. Does every family member agree that this dog should be a member of the family?

3. How will you care for the puppy and, later, the adult dog, and what arrangements do you plan to make? Who will care for this dog if you become ill or are on holiday?

4. Can one member of the family be with your Bernese for the most part of every day?

5. Will you object to the dust, dirt and hair that a normal Bernese will drag through your home?

6. Do you have enough house and outdoor space suitable for this large breed of dog?

7. Does your landlord or homeowner association allow the keeping of large dogs as pets?

8. Can you afford the food, health care, supplies and other costs that come with the dog?

9. Do any family members suffer from allergies to dog hair?

10. Are you committed to all of the above for the next ten years?

Consider the needs of the dog before acquiring a Bernese Mountain Dog. This dog will depend on you for everything from food and water to exercise, entertainment and affection.

INTRODUCTION TO
THE BREED STANDARD

Every breed that is recognised by a national or international breed registry is judged against what is called a breed standard; that is, a detailed description of the dog's physical characteristics, natural ability and temperament. Most standards were written and approved by the original breed fanciers who initiated the dog's acceptance into The Kennel Club or other registry. Their goal was to describe the ideal specimen of their breed, and the standard is intended to be a guideline for judging in the show ring. This is equally important as a blueprint for the breeding of future genera-

tions of each breed. Without such guidelines, specific inherent breed qualities could be changed, lost or completely eliminated. While it is not possible to produce a perfect specimen of any breed, breeders who respect and understand their standard will continue to select and breed only the best representatives of their particular breed.

THE KENNEL CLUB STANDARD FOR THE BERNESE MOUNTAIN DOG

General Appearance: Strong, sturdy working dog, active, alert, well boned, of striking colour.

Characteristics: A multi-purpose farm dog capable of draught work. A kind and devoted family dog. Slow to mature.

Temperament: Self-confident, good-natured, friendly and fearless. Aggressiveness not to be tolerated.

Head and Skull: Strong with flat skull, very slight furrow, well defined stop; strong straight muzzle. Lips slightly developed.

BREEDER'S BLUEPRINT

If you are considering breeding your bitch, it is very important that you are familiar with the breed standard. Reputable breeders breed with the intention of producing dogs that are as close as possible to the standard and contribute to the advancement of the breed. Study the standard for both physical appearance and temperament, and make certain your bitch and your chosen stud dog measure up.

Eyes: Dark brown, almond-shaped, well fitting eyelids.

Ears: Medium-sized; set high, triangular-shaped, lying flat in repose, when alert brought slightly forward and raised at base.

Mouth: Jaws strong with a perfect, regular and complete scissor bite, i.e. upper teeth closely overlapping lower teeth and set square to the jaws.

Neck: Strong, muscular and medium length.

Forequarters: Shoulders long, strong and sloping, with upper arm forming a distinct angle, flat lying, well muscled. Forelegs straight from all sides. Pasterns flexing slightly.

Body: Compact rather than long. Height to length 9:10. Broad chest, good depth of brisket reaching at least to elbow. Well ribbed; strong loins. Firm, straight back. Rump smoothly rounded.

Hindquarters: Broad, strong and well muscled. Stifles well bent. Hock strong, well let down and turning neither in nor out. Dewclaws to be removed.

Feet: Short, round and compact.

Tail: Bushy, reaching just below hock. Raised when alert or moving but never curled or carried over back.

Gait/Movement: Stride reaching out well in front, following well through behind, balanced stride in all gaits.

Coat: Soft, silky with bright natural sheen, long, slightly wavy but should not curl when mature.

The characteristic strong head with a flat skull is desirable in the Berner.

The strong body, compact rather than long, is called for in the breed standard.

The desirable tri-colour pattern must have a white blaze on the head and a white cross on the chest.

Colour: Jet black, with rich reddish-brown on cheeks, over eyes, on all four legs and on chest. Slight to medium-sized symmetrical white head marking (blaze) and white chest marking (cross) are essential. Preferred but not essential, white paws, white not reaching higher than pastern, white tip to tail. A few white hairs at nape of neck, and white anal patch undesirable but tolerated.

Size: Height: dogs: 64–70 cms (25–27.5 ins); bitches: 58–66 cms (23–26 ins).

THE IDEAL SPECIMEN

According to The Kennel Club, 'The Breed Standard is the "Blueprint" of the ideal specimen in each breed approved by a governing body, e.g. The Kennel Club, the Fédération Cynologique International (FCI) and the American Kennel Club.

'The Kennel Club writes and revises Breed Standards taking account of the advice of Breed Councils/Clubs. Breed Standards are not changed lightly to avoid "changing the standard to fit the current dogs" and the health and well-being of future dogs is always taken into account when new standards are prepared or existing ones altered.'

BREEDING CONSIDERATIONS

The decision to breed your dog is one that must be considered carefully and researched thoroughly before moving into action. Some people believe that breeding will make their bitch happier or that it is an easy way to make money. Unfortunately, indiscriminate breeding only worsens the rampant problem of pet overpopulation, as well as putting a considerable dent in your purse. As for the bitch, the entire process from mating through whelping is not an easy one and puts your pet under considerable stress. Last, but not least, consider whether or not you have the means to care for an entire litter of pups. Without a reputation in the field, your attempts to sell the pups may be unsuccessful.

Faults: Any departure from the foregoing points should be considered a fault and the seriousness with which the fault should be regarded should be in exact proportion to its degree.

Note: Male animals should have two apparently normal testicles fully descended into the scrotum.

PUPPY SELECTION

Your selection of a good puppy can be determined by your needs. A show potential or a good pet? It is your choice. Every puppy, however, should be of good temperament. Although show-quality puppies are bred and raised with emphasis on physical conformation, responsible breeders strive for equally good temperament. Do not buy from a breeder who concentrates solely on physical beauty at the expense of personality.

SELECTING YOUR BERNESE PUPPY

Unless you plan to show your Bernese, selecting for health and temperament will be more important than the puppy's colour or markings. A typical Bernese puppy should look square and solid and should carry a thick fuzzy coat. A teddy-bear-shaped head is preferable to a fox-like appearance. Healthy pups will have clear eyes, sound structure and correct dentition. The sire and dam should have the necessary clearances for hips, elbows and eyes. It is also wise to visit with and observe at least one of the parents before committing to a pup.

However, the most important consideration in selecting your Bernese is to obtain him as a pup or at least before about one year of age. As a guarding breed with a strong need to be with his people, the Bernese has difficulty coping with a change in owners later in life. Major late-life changes can make him extremely overanxious, disobedient, rebellious and even aggressive. It is best for both dog and human that bonds be established early in the dog's life.

HEREDITARY DISEASES THAT CONCERN PUPPY BUYERS

The Bernese Mountain Dog, unfortunately, does not enjoy the longevity of many other pure-bred dogs, which is all the more reason for potential owners to be concerned about the breed's hereditary diseases. When you meet with your chosen breeder, you should ask him about the diseases discussed herein.

Responsible breeders screen their dogs for hereditary problems before including them in their breeding programmes. Since these problems are passed directly from parents to puppies, whether as carriers or as affected animals, breeders must make screening a priority in their programmes. If the breeder you've selected has no interest or concern in these hereditary diseases, find another breeder. Your investment of time in finding a healthy litter of Bernese puppies can pay

DID YOU KNOW?
You should not even think about buying a puppy that looks sick, undernourished, overly frightened or nervous. Sometimes a timid puppy will warm up to you after a 30-minute 'let's-get-acquainted' session.

off in added years with your beloved pet in the future.

HIP DYSPLASIA (HD)

Hip dysplasia is an hereditary disease that involves abnormal or poor formation of the hip joint. Affecting many large-breed dogs, a mild case of HD can cause painful arthritis in the average housedog, and a severe case can render a working dog useless at his designated task. Diagnosis is made only through x-ray examination by a veterinary surgeon, and in

BOY OR GIRL?
An important consideration to be discussed is the sex of your puppy. For a family companion, a bitch may be the better choice, considering the female's inbred concern for all young creatures and her accompanying tolerance and patience. It is always advisable to spay a pet bitch, which may guarantee her a longer life.

DO YOU KNOW ABOUT HIP DYSPLASIA?

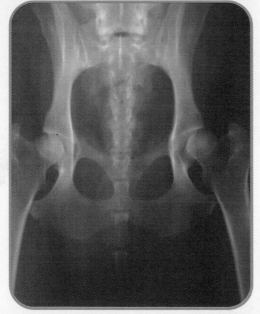

X-ray of a dog with 'Good' hips.

X-ray of a dog with 'Moderate' dysplastic hips.

Hip dysplasia is a fairly common condition found in purebred dogs. When a dog has hip dysplasia, its hind leg has an incorrectly formed hip joint. By constant use of the hip joint, it becomes more and more loose, wears abnormally and may become arthritic.

Hip dysplasia can only be confirmed with an x-ray, but certain symptoms may indicate a problem. Your dog may have a hip dysplasia problem if it walks in a peculiar manner, hops instead of smoothly runs, uses its hind legs in unison (to keep the pressure off the weak joint), has trouble getting up from a prone position or always sits with both legs together on one side of its body.

As the dog matures, it may adapt well to life with a bad hip, but in a few years the arthritis develops and many dogs with hip dysplasia become cripples.

Hip dysplasia is considered an inherited disease and only can be diagnosed definitively when the dog is two years old. Some experts claim that a special diet might help your puppy outgrow the bad hip, but the usual treatments are surgical. The removal of the pectineus muscle, the removal of the round part of the femur, reconstructing the pelvis and replacing the hip with an artificial one are all surgical interventions that are expensive, but they are usually very successful. Follow the advice of your veterinary surgeon.

Switzerland and the UK, this may be done only after the dog is at least one year of age.

In the USA, permanent grades are not assigned until the dog is two years old. Despite the hip guidelines and grading used in breeding programmes in the USA, 28 percent of Bernese hip x-rays submitted for evaluation in that country are rated as dysplastic. Berners have the eighth highest incidence of HD in the USA, and it is believed that the overall incidence is in reality much higher, since poor hip x-rays are seldom submitted for evaluation.

In Great Britain, the British Veterinary Association and The Kennel Club (BVA/KC) evaluate the x-rays and assign a score of 0 (which is the minimum or best possible score) up to 53 (the worst possible score) for each hip, producing possible total scores of 0 to 106.

Switzerland and Germany have strict rules, allowing only dogs with grades of 0 or 1 to be bred, which has significantly reduced the incidence of HD in those countries. But since the genetic predisposition is very complex, with many genes involved, there is little likelihood that the disease can be completely eliminated.

OSTEOCHONDRITIS DISSECANS (OCD)
Similar to HD, OCD affects the joints of the shoulder, elbow, hock

PUPPY APPEARANCE
Your puppy should have a well-fed appearance but not a distended abdomen, which may indicate worms or incorrect feeding, or both. The body should be firm, with a solid feel. The skin of the abdomen should be pale pink and clean, without signs of scratching or rash. Check the hind legs to make certain that dewclaws were removed, if any were present at birth.

DOCUMENTATION

Two important documents you will get from the breeder are the pup's pedigree and registration certificate. The breeder should register the litter and each pup with The Kennel Club, and it is necessary for you to have the paperwork if you plan on showing or breeding in the future.

Make sure you know the breeder's intentions on which type of registration he will obtain for the pup. There are limited registrations which may prohibit the dog from being shown, bred or from competing in non-conformation trials such as Working or Agility if the breeder feels that the pup is not of sufficient quality to do so. There is also a type of registration that will permit the dog in non-conformation competition only.

On the reverse side of the registration certificate, the new owner can find the transfer section which must be signed by the breeder.

is identified through x-ray, and surgery is usually necessary to correct the problem. Males are generally more affected than females, perhaps due to the more rapid growth rate of the male animal. OCD tends to occur in certain families of dogs, with some lines producing higher incidences of the disease. Environmental factors are also thought to contribute to the onset of OCD, with diet and strenuous exercise heavily implicated as offenders.

HISTIOCYTOSIS

Histiocytosis is the most prevalent cancer in Bernese Mountain Dogs and is a common cause of early death. A histiocyte is a type of white blood cell that comprises part of the dog's immune system. These cells capture bacteria and other foreign material and dispose of them. In histiocytosis, the cells rapidly proliferate and invade major portions of the body tissue. The disease is inherited and there are no known cures or treatments; thus, detection of affected dogs is a priority in Bernese breeding programmes. The disease is rare in other breeds but is the most common cancer in the Bernese, comprising 25% of all cancer cases.

Two types of histiocytosis exist, malignant and systemic. Malignant involves the lymph nodes, spleen and liver, and is the

and stifle, with the shoulder and elbow the most commonly afflicted joints in the Bernese. The disease most commonly affects the growing joints of a puppy under one year of age, and pups will usually exhibit symptoms between five and eight months of age when they come up lame for no apparent reason. The condition

more aggressive form of the disease. Onset is sudden and usually leads to death with a few weeks.

Early symptoms include depression, lethargy, loss of appetite and weight loss. Skin abnormalities are not uncommon, especially on the face and limbs. There are no known cures or treatments, so the only recourse is to monitor the dog's quality of life to determine the appropriate time for euthanasia.

HYPOMYELINGENESIS (TREMBLER)

This inherited disease is a condition caused by a lack of myelin, which is the sheath of insulation material that covers the nerves of the spinal cord. In this disease, the nerve impulses do not travel to the desired destination and instead spread out along the way, causing involuntary trembling.

This condition becomes apparent at 10 to 14 days of age when the pups begin to stand and walk. Affected pups will bobble noticeably and trembling is quite exaggerated, becoming so rapid that it may not be readily discernible from a distance, although it is easily felt when the pup is held. The trembling can remain constant or it can be progressive, with some dogs becoming affected later or more seriously than is typical.

Thus far, this condition exists

PREPARING FOR PUP

Unfortunately, when a puppy is bought by someone who does not take into consideration the time and attention that dog ownership requires, it is the puppy who suffers when he is either abandoned or placed in a shelter by a frustrated owner. So all of the 'homework' you do in preparation for your pup's arrival will benefit you both. The more informed you are, the more you will know what to expect and the better equipped you will be to handle the ups and downs of raising a puppy. Hopefully, everyone in the household is willing to do his part in raising and caring for the pup. The anticipation of owning a dog often brings a lot of promises from excited family members: 'I will walk him every day,' 'I will feed him,' 'I will house-train him,' etc., but these things take time and effort, and promises can easily be forgotten once the novelty of the new pet has worn off.

INSURANCE

Many good breeders will offer you insurance with your new puppy, which is an excellent idea. The first few weeks of insurance will probably be covered free of charge or with only minimal cost, allowing you to take up the policy when this expires. If you own a pet dog, it is sensible to take out such a policy as veterinary fees can be high, although routine vaccinations and boosters are not covered. Look carefully at the many options open to you before deciding which suits you best.

only in the UK. The disease has been traced to a Bernese named Duntiblac Nalle, a Swedish import who is the apparent common ancestor and first known carrier. Carriers can be identified only when bred to another carrier and affected puppies are produced. Carriers are normal, unaffected dogs, showing no signs of carrying the bad gene, and thus many carriers are unrecognised. It is known that carrier dogs have been exported to other countries, which could introduce the problem elsewhere. Outcrossing Nalle descendants will prevent producing affected pups, but can still produce carriers. The responsibility lies heavily on the breeders' shoulders.

COMMITMENT OF OWNERSHIP

After considering all of these factors, you have most likely already made some very important decisions about selecting your puppy. You have chosen a Bernese Mountain Dog, which means that you have decided which characteristics you want in a dog and what type of dog will best fit into your family and lifestyle. If you have selected a breeder, you have gone a step further—you have done your research and found a responsible, conscientious person who breeds quality Bernese and who should be a reliable source of help as you and your puppy adjust to life together. If you have observed a litter in action, you have obtained a firsthand look at the dynamics of a puppy 'pack' and, thus, you should learn about each pup's individual personality—perhaps you have even found one that

DID YOU KNOW?

Breeders rarely release puppies until they are eight to ten weeks of age. This is an acceptable age for most breeds of dog, excepting toy breeds, which are not released until around 12 weeks, given their petite sizes. If a breeder has a puppy that is 12 weeks or more, it is likely well socialised and house-trained. Be sure that it is otherwise healthy before deciding to take it home.

The friendly, smiling personality of the Bernese arrests you and owns you for a lifetime. Make your selection of your dog with care.

particularly appeals to you.

However, even if you have not yet found the Bernese puppy of your dreams, observing pups will help you learn to recognise certain behaviour and to determine what a pup's behaviour indicates about his temperament. You will be able to pick out which pups are the leaders, which ones are less outgoing, which ones are confident, which ones are shy, playful, friendly, aggressive, etc. Equally as important, you will learn to recognise what a healthy pup should look and act like. All of these things will help you in your search, and when you find the Berner that was meant for you, you will know it!

Researching your breed, selecting a responsible breeder and observing as many pups as possible are all important steps on the way to dog ownership. It may seem like a lot of effort...and you have not even taken the pup home yet! Remember, though, you cannot be too careful when it comes to deciding on the type of dog you want and finding out about your prospective pup's background. Buying a puppy is not—or should not be—just another whimsical purchase. This is one instance in which you actually do get to choose your own family! You may be thinking that buying a puppy should be fun—it should not be so serious and so much work. Keep in mind that your puppy is not a cuddly stuffed toy or decorative lawn ornament, but a creature that will become a real member of your family. You will come to realise that, while buying a puppy is a pleasurable and exciting endeavour, it is not something to be taken lightly. Relax…the fun will start when the pup comes home!

Always keep in mind that a puppy is nothing more than a baby in a furry disguise…a baby who is virtually helpless in a human world and who trusts his owner for fulfilment of his basic needs for survival. In addition to water and shelter, your pup needs care, protection, guidance and love. If you are not prepared to commit to this, then you are not prepared to own a dog.

Wait a minute, you say. How hard could this be? All of my neighbours own dogs and they seem to be doing just fine. Why should I have to worry about all of this? Well, you should not worry about it; in fact, you will probably find that once your Bernese pup gets used to his new home, he will fall into his place in the family quite naturally. But it never hurts to emphasise the commitment of dog ownership. With some time and patience, it is really not too difficult to raise a curious and exuberant Bernese pup to be a well-adjusted and well-mannered adult dog—a dog that could be your most loyal friend.

PREPARING PUPPY'S PLACE IN YOUR HOME

Researching your breed and finding a breeder are only two aspects of the 'homework' you will have to do before taking your Bernese puppy home. You will also have to prepare your home and family for the new addition. Much as you would prepare a nursery for a newborn baby, you will need to designate a place in your home that will be the puppy's own. How you prepare your home will depend on how much freedom the dog will be allowed. Whatever you decide, you must ensure that he has a place that he can 'call his own.'

When you bring your new puppy into your home, you are bringing him into what will become his home as well. Obviously, you did not buy a puppy so that he could take over your house, but in order for a puppy to grow into a stable, well-adjusted dog, he has to feel

ARE YOU A FIT OWNER?
If the breeder from whom you are buying a puppy asks you a lot of personal questions, do not be insulted. Such a breeder wants to be sure that you will be a fit provider for his puppy.

comfortable in his surroundings. Remember, he is leaving the warmth and security of his mother and littermates, as well as the familiarity of the only place he has ever known, so it is important to make his transition as easy as possible. By preparing a place in your home for the puppy, you are making him feel as welcome as possible in a strange new place. It should not take him long to get used to it, but the sudden shock of being transplanted is somewhat traumatic for a young pup. Imagine how a small child would feel in the same situation—that is how your puppy must be feeling. It is up to you to reassure him and to let him know, 'Little chap, you are going to like it here!'

WHAT YOU SHOULD BUY

CRATE

To someone unfamiliar with the use of crates in dog training, it may seem like punishment to shut a dog in a crate, but this is not the case at all. Although all breeders do not advocate crate training, more and more breeders and trainers are recommending crates as preferred tools for show puppies as well as pet puppies. Crates are not cruel—crates have many humane and highly effective uses in dog care and training. For example, crate training is a very popular and

YOUR SCHEDULE . . .
If you lead an erratic, unpredictable life, with daily or weekly changes in your work requirements, consider the problems of owning a puppy. The new puppy has to be fed regularly, socialised (loved, petted, handled, introduced to other people) and, most importantly, allowed to visit outdoors for toilet training. As the dog gets older, it can be more tolerant of deviations in its feeding and toilet relief.

very successful house-training method. A crate can keep your dog safe during travel and, perhaps most importantly, a crate provides your dog with a place of his own in your home. It serves as a 'doggie bedroom' of sorts—your Bernese can curl up in his crate when he wants to sleep or when he just needs a break. Many dogs

PHOTO COURTESY OF DOSKOCIL

As far as purchasing a crate, the type that you buy is up to you. It will most likely be one of the two most popular types: wire or fibreglass. There are advantages and disadvantages to each type. For example, a wire crate is more open, allowing the air to flow through and affording the dog a view of what is going on around him, while a fibreglass crate is sturdier. Both can double as travel crates, providing protection for the dog. The size of the crate is another thing to consider. Puppies do not stay puppies forever—in fact, sometimes it seems as if they grow right before your eyes. A small crate may be fine for a very young Bernese pup, but it will not do him much good for long! Unless you have the money and the inclination to buy a new crate every time your pup has a growth spurt, it is better to get one that will accommodate your dog both as a pup and at full size. At 75 to 100 pounds as an adult, your Berner will require and extra-large crate, 24–26 inches wide and 38–52 inches long.

Crates of various sizes are available at your local pet shop. Purchase a crate large enough for a fully-grown Berner.

sleep in their crates overnight. With soft bedding and his favourite toy, a crate becomes a cosy pseudo-den for your dog. Like his ancestors, he too will seek out the comfort and retreat of a den—you just happen to be providing him with something a little more luxurious than what his early ancestors enjoyed.

BEDDING
Veterinary bedding in the dog's crate will help the dog feel more at home and you may also like to pop in a small blanket. This will take the place of the leaves, twigs, etc., that the pup would use in the wild to make a den; the pup can make his own 'burrow' in the

crate. Although your pup is far removed from his den-making ancestors, the denning instinct is still a part of his genetic makeup. Second, until you take your pup home, he has been sleeping amidst the warmth of his mother and littermates, and while a blanket is not the same as a warm, breathing body, it still provides heat and something with which to snuggle. You will want to wash your pup's bedding frequently in case he has an 'accident' in his crate, and replace or remove any blanket that becomes ragged and starts to fall apart.

TOYS

Toys are a must for dogs of all ages, especially for curious playful pups. Puppies are the 'children' of the dog world, and what child does not love toys? Chew toys provide enjoyment for both dog and owner—your dog will enjoy playing with his favourite toys, while you will enjoy the fact that they distract him from your expensive shoes and leather sofa. Puppies love to chew; in fact, chewing is a physical need for pups as they are teething, and everything looks appetising! The full range of your possessions—from old tea towel to Oriental carpet—are fair game in the eyes of a teething pup. Puppies are not all that discerning when it comes to finding something to literally 'sink their

CRATE TRAINING TIPS

During crate training, you should partition off the section of the crate in which the pup stays. If he is given too big an area, this will hinder your training efforts. Crate training is based on the fact that a dog does not like to soil his sleeping quarters, so it is ineffective to keep a pup in a crate that is so big that he can eliminate in one end and get far enough away from it to sleep. Also, you want to make the crate den-like for the pup. Blankets and a favourite toy will make the crate cosy for the small pup; as he grows, you may want to evict some of his 'roommates' to make more room.

It will take some coaxing at first, but be patient. Given some time to get used to it, your pup will adapt to his new home-within-a-home quite nicely.

TOYS, TOYS, TOYS!

With a big variety of dog toys available, and so many that look like they would be a lot of fun for a dog, be careful in your selection. It is amazing what a set of puppy teeth can do to an innocent-looking toy, so, obviously, safety is a major consideration. Be sure to choose the most durable products that you can find. Hard nylon bones and toys are a safe bet, and many of them are offered in different scents and flavours that will be sure to capture your dog's attention. It is always fun to play a game of catch with your dog, and there are balls and flying discs that are specially made to withstand dog teeth.

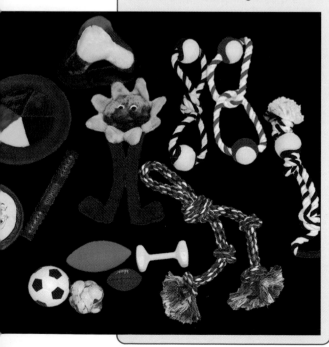

teeth into'—everything tastes great!

Bernese puppies are fairly active chewers and only the safest toys should be offered to them. Breeders advise owners to resist stuffed toys, because they can become de-stuffed in no time. The overly excited pup may ingest the stuffing, which can cause stomach problems.

Similarly, squeaky toys are quite popular, but must be avoided for the Bernese. Perhaps a squeaky toy can be used as an aid in training, but not for free play. If a pup 'disembowels' one of these, the small plastic squeaker inside can be dangerous if swallowed. Monitor the condition of all your pup's toys carefully and get rid of any that have been chewed to the point of becoming potentially dangerous.

Be careful of natural bones, which have a tendency to splinter into sharp, dangerous pieces. Also be careful of rawhide, which can turn into pieces that are easy to swallow and become a mushy mess on your carpet.

LEAD

A nylon lead is probably the best option as it is the most resistant to puppy teeth should your pup take a liking to chewing on his lead. Of course, this is a habit that should be nipped in the bud, but if your pup likes to chew on his lead he has a very slim chance of being

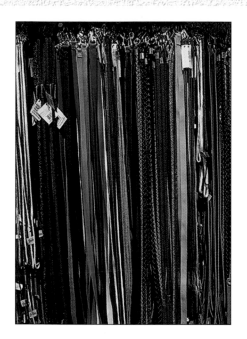

Your local pet shop will surely have a large array of leads from which you can select the leads which best suit your needs. The training lead will usually differ from the lead used when the dog is fully trained to heel.

MENTAL AND DENTAL

Toys not only help your puppy get the physical and mental stimulation he needs but also provide a great way to keep his teeth clean. Hard rubber or nylon toys, especially those constructed with grooves, are designed to scrape away plaque, preventing bad breath and gum infection.

able to chew through the strong nylon. Nylon leads are also lightweight, which is good for a young Bernese who is just getting used to the idea of walking on a lead.

TEETHING TIP

Puppies like soft toys for chewing. Because they are teething, soft items like stuffed toys soothe their aching gums.

For everyday walking and safety purposes, the nylon lead is a good choice. As your pup grows up and gets used to walking on the lead, you may want to purchase a flexible lead. These leads allow you to extend the length to give the dog a broader area to explore or to shorten the length to keep the dog near you. Of course there are special leads for training purposes, and

PHOTO COURTESY OF MIKKI PET PRODUCTS.

specially made leather harnesses, but these are not necessary for routine walks.

COLLAR

Your pup should get used to wearing a collar all the time since you will want to attach his ID tags to it, plus you have to attach the lead to something! A lightweight nylon collar is a good choice; make sure that it fits snugly enough so that the pup cannot wriggle out of it, but is loose enough so that it will not be uncomfortably tight around the pup's neck. You should be able to fit a finger between the pup and the collar. It may take some time for your pup to get used to wearing the collar, but soon he will not even notice that it is there. Choke collars are made for training, but should only be used by an experienced handler.

FOOD AND WATER BOWLS

Your pup will need two bowls, one for food and one for water. You may want two sets of bowls, one for inside and one for outside, depending on where the dog will be fed and where he will be spending time. Stainless steel or sturdy plastic bowls are popular choices. Plastic bowls are more chewable. Dogs tend not to chew on the steel variety, which can be sterilised. It is important to buy sturdy bowls since anything is in danger of being chewed by puppy teeth and you do not want your

CHOOSE AN APPROPRIATE COLLAR

The BUCKLE COLLAR is the standard collar used for everyday purpose. Be sure that you adjust the buckle on growing puppies. Check it every day. It can become too tight overnight! These collars can be made of leather or nylon. Attach your dog's identification tags to this collar.

The CHOKE COLLAR is the usual collar recommended for training. It is constructed of highly polished steel so that it slides easily through the stainless steel loop. The idea is that the dog controls the pressure around its neck and he will stop pulling if the collar becomes uncomfortable. Never leave a choke collar on your dog when not training.

The HALTER is for a trained dog that has to be restrained to prevent running away, chasing a cat and the like. Considered the most humane of all collars, it is frequently used on smaller dogs for which collars are not comfortable.

Your local pet shop will have suitable aids to assist you in cleaning up after your Bernese Mountain Dog has relieved itself.

dog to be constantly chewing apart his bowl (for his safety and for your purse!).

CLEANING SUPPLIES
Until a pup is house-trained you will be doing a lot of cleaning. Accidents will occur, which is acceptable in the beginning because the puppy does not know any better. All you can do is be prepared to clean up any 'accidents.' Old rags, towels, newspapers and a safe disinfectant are good to have on hand.

BEYOND THE BASICS
The items previously discussed are the bare necessities. You will find out what else you need as you go along—grooming supplies,

flea/tick protection, baby gates to partition a room, etc. These things will vary depending on your situation but it is important that you have everything you need to feed and make your Bernese comfortable in his first few days at home.

PUPPY-PROOFING YOUR HOME
Aside from making sure that your Bernese will be comfortable in your home, you also have to make sure that your home is safe for your Bernese. This means taking precautions that your pup will not get into anything he should not get into and that there is nothing within his reach that may harm him should he sniff it, chew it, inspect it, etc. This probably seems obvious since, while you

---

FINANCIAL RESPONSIBILITY
Grooming tools, collars, leashes, dog beds and, of course, toys will be an expense to you when you first obtain your pup, and the cost will continue throughout your dog's lifetime. If your puppy damages or destroys your possessions (as most puppies surely will!) or something belonging to a neighbour, you can calculate additional expense. There is also flea and pest control, which every dog owner faces more than once. You must be able to handle the financial responsibility of owning a dog.

are primarily concerned with your pup's safety, at the same time you do not want your belongings to be ruined. Breakables should be placed out of reach if your dog is to have full run of the house. If he is to be limited to certain places within the house, keep any potentially dangerous items in the 'off-limits' areas. An electrical cord can pose a danger should the puppy decide to taste it—and who is going to convince a pup that it would not make a great chew toy? Cords should be fastened tightly against the wall. If your dog is going to spend time in a crate, make sure that there is nothing near his crate that he can reach if he sticks his curious little nose or paws through the openings. Just as you would with a child, keep all household cleaners and

THE RIDE HOME

Taking your dog from the breeder to your home in a car can be a very uncomfortable experience for both of you. The puppy will have been taken from his warm, friendly, safe environment and brought into a strange new environment. An environment that moves! Be prepared for loose bowels, urination, crying, whining and even fear biting. With proper love and encouragement when you arrive home, the stress of the trip should quickly disappear.

PLAY'S THE THING

Teaching the puppy to play with his toys in running and fetching games is an ideal way to help the puppy develop muscle, learn motor skills and bond with you, his owner and master.

He also needs to learn how to inhibit his bite reflex and never to use his teeth on people, forbidden objects and other animals in play. Whenever you play with your puppy, you make the rules. This becomes an important message to your puppy in teaching him that you are the pack leader and control everything he does in life. Once your dog accepts you as his leader, your relationship with him will be cemented for life.

TOXIC PLANTS

Many plants can be toxic to dogs. If you see your dog carrying a piece of vegetation in his mouth, approach him in a quiet, disinterested manner, avoid eye contact, pet him and gradually remove the plant from his mouth. Alternatively, offer him a treat and maybe he'll drop the plant on his own accord. Be sure no toxic plants are growing in your own garden.

climbing fences or digging under them, although a bored Berner may dig holes out of frustration. A five- to six-foot fence, well-embedded into the ground, is recommended to keep your Bernese safe.

FIRST TRIP TO THE VET

You have selected your puppy, and your home and family are ready. Now all you have to do is collect your Berner from the breeder and the fun begins, right? Well...not so fast. Something else you need to prepare is your pup's first trip to the veterinary surgeon. Perhaps the breeder can recommend someone in the area

chemicals where the pup cannot reach them.

It is also important to make sure that the outside of your home is safe. Of course your puppy should never be unsupervised, but a pup let loose in the garden will want to run and explore, and he should be granted that freedom. Berners are not known for

PUPPY-PROOFING

Thoroughly puppy-proof your house before bringing your puppy home. Never use roach or rodent poisons in any area accessible to the puppy. Avoid the use of toilet cleaners. Most dogs are born with 'toilet sonar' and will take a drink if the lid is left open. Also keep the rubbish secured and out of reach.

who specialises in large-breed dogs or maybe you know some other Bernese owners who can suggest a good vet. Either way, you should have an appointment arranged for your pup before you pick him up.

The pup's first visit will consist of an overall examination to make sure that the pup does not have any problems that are not apparent to the owner. The veterinary surgeon will also set up a schedule for the pup's vaccinations; the breeder will inform you of which ones the pup has already

Berner puppies are curious and active, ready to investigate every centimetre of your garden. Be on guard when your puppy is roaming about your grounds to make sure all is safe for his inspection.

CHEMICAL TOXINS

Scour your garage for potential puppy dangers. Remove weed killers, pesticides and antifreeze materials. Antifreeze is highly toxic and even a few drops can kill a dog. The sweet taste attracts the animal, who will quickly consume it from the floor or curbside.

NATURAL TOXINS

Examine your grass and garden landscaping before bringing your puppy home. Many varieties of plants have leaves, stems or flowers that are toxic if ingested, and you can depend on a curious puppy to investigate them. Ask your vet for information on poisonous plants or research them at your library.

received and the vet can continue from there.

INTRODUCTION TO THE FAMILY

Everyone in the house will be excited about the puppy coming home and will want to pet him and play with him, but it is best to make the introduction low-key so as not to overwhelm the puppy. He is apprehensive already. It is the first time he has been separated from his mother and the breeder, and the ride to your home is likely to be the first time he has been in a car. The last thing you want to do is smother him, as this will only frighten him further. This is not to say that human contact is not extremely necessary at this stage, because this is the time when a connection between the pup and his human family is formed. Gentle petting and soothing words should help console him, as well as just putting him down and letting him explore on his own (under your watchful eye, of course).

The pup may approach the family members or may busy himself with exploring for a while. Gradually, each person should spend some time with the pup, one at a time, crouching down to get as close to the pup's level as possible and letting him sniff their hands and petting him gently. He definitely needs human attention and he needs to be touched—this is how to form an immediate bond. Just remember that the pup is experiencing a lot of things for the first time, at the same time. There are new people, new noises, new smells and new things to investigate: so be gentle, be affectionate and be as comforting as you can be.

PUP'S FIRST NIGHT HOME

You have travelled home with your new charge safely in his crate. He's been to the vet for a thorough check-up; he's been weighed, his papers examined; perhaps he's even been vaccinated and wormed as well. He's met the family, licked the whole family, including the excited children and the less-than-happy cat. He's explored his area, his new bed, the garden and anywhere else he's

Properly socialised, Berners will happily make the acquaintance of your house cat, particularly if your cat is smartly tri-coloured like this delightful Swiss kitty.

been permitted. He's eaten his first meal at home and relieved himself in the proper place. He's heard lots of new sounds, smelled new friends and seen more of the outside world than ever before.

That was just the first day! He's worn out and is ready for bed...or so you think!

It's puppy's first night and you are ready to say 'Good night'— keep in mind that this is puppy's first night ever to be sleeping alone. His dam and littermates are no longer at paw's length and he's a bit scared, cold and lonely. Be reassuring to your new family member. This is not the time to spoil him and give in to his inevitable whining.

Puppies whine. They whine to let others know where they are and hopefully to get company out of it. Place your pup in his new bed or crate in his room and close the door. Mercifully, he may fall asleep without a peep. When the inevitable occurs, ignore the whining: he is fine. Be strong and keep his interest in mind. Do not allow yourself to feel guilty and visit the pup. He will fall asleep eventually.

Many breeders recommend placing a piece of bedding from his former home in his new bed so that he recognises the scent of his littermates. Others still advise placing a hot water bottle in his bed for warmth. This latter may be a good idea provided the pup

A FORTNIGHT'S GRACE
It will take at least two weeks for your puppy to become accustomed to his new surroundings. Give him lots of love, attention, handling, frequent opportunities to relieve himself, a diet he likes to eat and a place he can call his own.

doesn't attempt to suckle—he'll get good and wet and may not fall asleep so fast.

Puppy's first night can be somewhat stressful for the pup and his new family. Remember that you are setting the tone of nighttime at your house. Unless you want to play with your pup every evening at 10 p.m., midnight and 2 a.m., don't initiate the habit. Your family will thank you, and so will your pup!

PREVENTING PUPPY PROBLEMS

SOCIALISATION

Now that you have done all of the preparatory work and have helped your pup get accustomed to his new home and family, it is about time for you to have some fun! Socialising your Bernese pup gives you the opportunity to show off your new friend, and your pup gets to reap the benefits of being an adorable furry creature that people will want to pet and, in general, think is absolutely precious!

Besides getting to know his new family, your puppy should be exposed to other people, animals and situations, but he must not come into close contact with dogs you don't know well until his course of injections is fully complete. This will help him become well adjusted as he grows up and less prone to being timid or fearful of the new things he will encounter. Your pup's socialisation began with the breeder but now it is your responsibility to continue it. The socialisation he receives up until the age of 12 weeks is the most critical, as this is the time when he forms his impressions of the outside world. Be especially careful during the eight-to-ten-week period, also

Socialisation of your Berner as a puppy will ensure safe behaviour as an adult. Dogs that have not been socialised properly can become overly shy or aggressive with other dogs.

known as the fear period. The interaction he receives during this time should be gentle and reassuring. Lack of socialisation can manifest itself in fear and aggression as the dog grows up. He needs lots of human contact, affection, handling and exposure to other animals.

Once your pup has received his necessary vaccinations, feel free to take him out and about (on his lead, of course). Walk him around the neighbourhood, take him on your daily errands, let people pet him, let him meet other dogs and pets, etc. Puppies do not have to try to make friends; there will be no shortage of people who will want to introduce themselves. Just make sure that you carefully supervise each meeting. If the neighbourhood children want to say hello,

SOCIALISATION

Thorough socialisation includes not only meeting new people but also being introduced to new experiences such as riding in the car, having his coat brushed, hearing the television, walking in a crowd—the list is endless. The more your pup experiences, and the more positive the experiences are, the less of a shock and the less frightening it will be for your pup to encounter new things.

for example, that is great— children and pups most often make great companions. Sometimes an excited child can unintentionally handle a pup too roughly, or an overzealous pup can playfully nip a little too hard. You want to make socialisation experiences positive ones. What a pup learns during this very formative stage will affect his attitude toward future encounters. You want your dog to be comfortable around everyone. A pup that has a bad experience with a child may grow up to be a dog that is shy around or aggressive toward children.

FEEDING TIP
You will probably start feeding your pup the same food that he has been getting from the breeder; the breeder should give you a few days' supply to start you off. Although you should not give your pup too many treats, you will want to have puppy treats on hand for coaxing, training, rewards, etc. Be careful, though, as a small pup's calorie requirements are relatively low and a few treats can add up to almost a full day's worth of calories without the required nutrition.

CONSISTENCY IN TRAINING
Dogs, being pack animals, naturally need a leader, or else they try to establish dominance in their packs. When you welcome a

PROPER SOCIALISATION

The socialisation period for puppies is from age 8 to 16 weeks. This is the time when puppies need to leave their birth family and take up residence with their new owners, where they will meet many new people, other pets, etc. Failure to be adequately socialised can cause the dog to grow up fearing others and being shy and unfriendly due to a lack of self-confidence.

Be sure you have your puppy's attention before giving a command. Nothing is more pressing to a puppy than an itch!

and cannot do. Do not give in to those pleading eyes—stand your ground when it comes to

dog into your family, the choice of who becomes the leader and who becomes the 'pack' is entirely up to you! Your pup's intuitive quest for dominance, coupled with the fact that it is nearly impossible to look at an adorable Bernese pup with his 'puppy-dog' eyes and not cave in, give the pup almost an unfair advantage in getting the upper hand! A pup will definitely test the waters to see what he can

disciplining the pup and make sure that all family members do the same. It will only confuse the pup when Mother tells him to get off the sofa when he is used to sitting up there with Father to watch the nightly news. Avoid discrepancies by having all members of the household decide on the rules before the pup even comes home...and be consistent in enforcing them! Early training shapes the dog's personality, so you cannot be unclear in what you expect.

COMMON PUPPY PROBLEMS

The best way to prevent puppy problems is to be proactive in stopping an undesirable behaviour as soon as it starts. The old saying 'You can't teach an old dog new tricks' does not necessarily hold true, but it is true that it is much easier to discourage bad behaviour in a young developing pup than to wait until the pup's bad behaviour becomes the adult dog's bad habit. There are some problems that are especially prevalent in puppies as they develop.

NO CHOCOLATE!

Use treats to bribe your dog into a desired behaviour. Try small pieces of hard cheese or freeze-dried liver. Never offer chocolate as it has toxic qualities for dogs.

MANNERS MATTER

During the socialisation process, a puppy should meet people, experience different environments and definitely be exposed to other canines. Through playing and interacting with other dogs, your puppy will learn lessons, ranging from controlling the pressure of his jaws by biting his littermates to the inner-workings of the canine pack that he will apply to his human relationships for the rest of his life. That is why removing a puppy from its litter too early (before eight weeks) can be detrimental to the pup's development.

NIPPING

As puppies start to teethe, they feel the need to sink their teeth into anything available...unfortunately that includes your fingers, arms, hair and toes. You may find this behaviour cute for the first five seconds...until you feel just how sharp those puppy teeth are. This is something you want to discourage immediately and consistently with a firm 'No!' (or whatever number of firm 'No's it takes for him to understand that you mean business). Then replace your finger with an appropriate chew toy. While this behaviour is merely annoying when the dog is young, it can become dangerous as your Bernese's adult teeth grow in and his jaws develop, and he continues to think it is okay to gnaw on human appendages. Your Bernese does not mean any harm with a friendly nip, but he also does not know his own strength.

The Berner puppy makes an attentive student who quickly absorbs commands and exercises, when the trainer is confident and clear in her desires.

CRYING/WHINING

Your pup will often cry, whine, whimper, howl or make some

type of commotion when he is left alone. This is basically his way of calling out for attention to make sure that you know he is there and that you have not forgotten about him. He feels insecure when he is left alone, when you are out of the house and he is in his crate or when you are in another part of the house and he cannot see you. The noise he is making is an expression of the anxiety he feels at being alone, so he needs to be taught that being alone is okay. You are not actually training the dog to stop making noise, you are training him to feel comfortable when he is alone and thus removing the need for him to make the noise. This is where the crate with cosy bedding and a toy comes in handy. You want to know that he is safe when you are not there to supervise, and you know that he will be safe in his crate rather than roaming freely about the house. In order

INHERIT THE MIND

In order to know whether or not a puppy will fit into your lifestyle, you need to assess his personality. A good way to do this is to interact with his parents. Your pup inherits not only his appearance but also his personality and temperament from the sire and dam. If the parents are fearful or overly aggressive, these same traits may likely show up in your puppy.

CHEWING TIPS

Chewing goes hand in hand with nipping in the sense that a teething puppy is always looking for a way to soothe his aching gums. In this case, instead of chewing on you, he may have taken a liking to your favourite shoe or something else which he should not be chewing. Again, realise that this is a normal canine behaviour that does not need to be discouraged, only redirected. Your pup just needs to be taught what is acceptable to chew on and what is off limits. Consistently tell him 'NO' when you catch him chewing on something forbidden and give him a chew toy. Conversely, praise him when you catch him chewing on something appropriate. In this way you are discouraging the inappropriate behaviour and reinforcing the desired behaviour. The puppy chewing should stop after his adult teeth have come in, but an adult dog continues to chew for various reasons—perhaps because he is bored, perhaps to relieve tension or perhaps he just likes to chew. That is why it is important to redirect his chewing when he is still young.

for the pup to stay in his crate without making a fuss, he needs to be comfortable in his crate. On that note, it is extremely important that the crate is never used as a form of punishment, or the pup will have a negative association with the crate.

Accustom the pup to the crate in short, gradually increasing time intervals in which you put him in the crate, maybe with a treat, and stay in the room with him. If he cries or makes a fuss, do not go to him, but stay in his sight. Gradually he will realise that staying in his crate is all right without your help, and it will not be so traumatic for him when you are not around. You may want to leave the radio on softly when you leave the house; the sound of human voices may be comforting to him.

DIETARY AND FEEDING CONSIDERATIONS

For years it was believed that large breeds of dogs required high-powered diets to support their rapid growth rates. This is not so today. It is now known that diets high in calories, primarily from fat and protein, actually contribute to skeletal problems during the first year of heavy growth. Veterinary nutritionists today recommend a balanced food that contains reduced amounts of fat and protein, and warn against supplementation with calcium and other vitamins, which could upset the balance of the food.

Today the choices of food for your Bernese are many and varied. There are simply dozens of brands of food in all sorts of flavours and textures, ranging from puppy diets to those for seniors. There are even hypoallergenic and low-calorie diets available. Because your Bernese's food has a bearing on coat, health and temperament, it is essential that the most suitable diet is selected for a Bernese of his age. It is fair to say, however, that even experienced owners can be perplexed by the enormous range of foods available. Only understanding what is best for your dog will help you reach a valued decision.

FEEDING TIP

You must store your dried dog food carefully. Open packages of dog food quickly lose their vitamin value, usually within 90 days of being opened. Mould spores and vermin could also contaminate the food.

Dog foods are produced in three basic types: dried, semi-moist and tinned. Dried foods are useful for the cost-conscious for overall they tend to be less expensive than semi-moist or tinned. They also contain the least fat and the most preservatives. In general, tinned foods are made up of 60–70 percent water, while semi-moist ones often contain so much sugar that they are perhaps the least preferred by owners, even though their dogs seem to like them.

When selecting your dog's diet, three stages of development must be considered: the puppy stage, adult stage and the senior or veteran stage.

PUPPY STAGE
Puppies instinctively want to suck milk from their mother's teats and a normal puppy will exhibit this behaviour from just a few moments following birth. If puppies do not attempt to suckle within the first half-hour or so, they should be encouraged to do so by placing them on the nipples, having selected ones with plenty of milk. This early milk supply is important in providing colostrum to protect the puppies during the first eight to ten weeks of their lives. Although a mother's milk is much better than any milk formula, despite there being some excellent ones available, if the puppies do not feed, the breeder will have to feed them himself. For those with less experience, advice

Owners must pay attention to their Berner's dentition. Brushing and checking for tooth decay are important parts of maintaining your dog's health.

TRAVEL TIP
Never leave your dog alone in the car. In hot weather your dog can die from the high temperature inside a closed vehicle; even a car parked in the shade can heat up very quickly. Leaving the window open is dangerous as well since the dog can hurt himself trying to get out.

small portions of suitable solid food. Most breeders like to introduce alternate milk and meat meals initially, building up to weaning time.

By the time the puppies are seven or a maximum of eight weeks old, they should be fully weaned and fed solely on a proprietary puppy food. Unless a special condition warrants it, Bernese pups should be fed a

Puppies are weaned by the time they are about eight weeks old. Breeders offer their puppies top-quality puppy food, and owners should continue using the same brand once the puppy comes to its new home.

from a veterinary surgeon is important so that not only the right quantity of milk is fed but that of correct quality, fed at suitably frequent intervals, usually every two hours during the first few days of life.

Puppies should be allowed to nurse from their mothers for about the first six weeks, although from the third or fourth week the breeder should begin to introduce

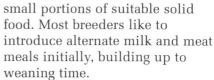

LET THE SUN SHINE
Your dog needs daily sunshine for the same reason people do. Pets kept inside homes with curtains drawn against the sun suffer from 'SAD' (Seasonal Affected Disorder) to the same degree as humans. We now know that sunlight must enter the iris and thus to the pineal gland to regulate the body's hormonal system and when we live and work in artificial light, both circadian rhythms and hormone balances are disturbed.

GRAIN-BASED DIETS
Some less expensive dog foods are based on grains and other plant proteins. While these products may appear to be attractively priced, many breeders prefer a diet based on animal proteins and believe that they are more conducive to your dog's health. Many grain-based diets rely on soy protein that may cause flatulence (passing gas).

There are many cases, however, when your dog might require a special diet. These special requirements should only be recommended by your veterinary surgeon.

TEST FOR PROPER DIET

A good test for proper diet is the colour, odour and firmness of your dog's stool. A healthy dog usually produces three semi-hard stools per day. The stools should have no unpleasant odour. They should be the same colour from excretion to excretion.

FOOD PREFERENCE

Selecting the best dried dog food is difficult. There is no majority consensus among veterinary scientists as to the value of nutrient analyses (protein, fat, fibre, moisture, ash, cholesterol, minerals, etc.). All agree that feeding trials are what matter, but you also have to consider the individual dog. Its weight, age, activity and what pleases its taste all must be considered. It is probably best to take the advice of your veterinary surgeon. Every dog's dietary requirements vary, even during the lifetime of a particular dog.

If your dog is fed a good dried food, it does not require supplements of meat or vegetables. Dogs do appreciate a little variety in their diets so you may choose to stay with the same brand, but vary the flavour. Alternatively, you may wish to add a little flavoured stock to give a difference to the taste.

high-quality diet designed specifically for large-breed pups during their first year. Owners should follow the advice of their vets when selecting the best puppy food for their Berners. Selection of the most suitable, good-quality diet at this time is essential, for a puppy's fastest growth rate is during the first year of life. Veterinary surgeons are usually able to offer advice in this regard and, although the frequency of meals will have been reduced over time, only when a young dog has reached the age of about 12 months should an adult diet be fed.

Puppy and junior diets should be well balanced for the needs of your dog, so that except in certain circumstances additional vitamins, minerals and proteins will not be required.

ADULT DIETS

Adult Berners should eat the same high-quality food, with adjusted levels of fat and protein according

TIPPING THE SCALES

Good nutrition is vital to your dog's health, but many people end up over-feeding or giving unnecessary supplements. Here are some common doggie diet don'ts:

- Adding milk, yoghurt and cheese to your dog's diet may seem like a good idea for coat and skin care, but dairy products are very fattening and can cause indigestion.
- Diets high in fat will not cause heart attacks in dogs but will certainly cause your dog to gain weight.
- Most importantly, don't assume your dog will simply stop eating once he doesn't need any more food. Given the chance, he will eat you out of house and home!

to each dog's individual activity level, metabolism and health condition. Great care should be taken to keep a Berner lean and well-muscled, as overweight dogs are more prone to joint disease and other health problems, which can affect the heart, kidneys and liver.

A dog is considered an adult when it has stopped growing, so in general the diet of a Bernese

THE CANINE GOURMET

Your dog does not prefer a fresh bone. Indeed, he wants it properly aged and, if given such a treat indoors, he is more likely to try to bury it in the carpet than he is to settle in for a good chew! If you have a garden, give him such delicacies outside and guide him to a place suitable for his 'bone yard.' He will carefully place the treasure in its earthy vault and seemingly forget about it. Trust me, his seeming distaste or lack of thanks for your thoughtfulness is not that at all. He will return in a few days to inspect it, perhaps to re-bury the thing, and when it is just right, he will relish it as much as you do that cooked-to-perfection steak. If he is in a concrete or bricked kennel run, he will be especially frustrated at the hopelessness of the situation. He will vacillate between ignoring it completely, giving it a few licks to speed the curing process with saliva and trying to hide it behind the water bowl! When the bone has aged a bit, he will set to work on it.

Mountain Dog can be changed to an adult one at about 12 months of age. Again you should rely upon your veterinary surgeon or dietary specialist to recommend an acceptable maintenance diet. Major dog food manufacturers specialise in this type of food, and it is merely necessary for you to select the one best suited to your dog's needs.

SENIOR DIETS

As dogs get older, their metabolism changes. The Berner should be considered a senior by around five to seven years of age, depending on the activity level of the dog. The older dog usually exercises less, moves more slowly and sleeps more. This change in lifestyle and physiological performance requires a change in diet. Since these changes take place slowly, they might not be recognisable. What is easily recognisable is weight gain. By continuing to feed your dog an adult-maintenance diet when it is slowing down metabolically, your dog will gain weight. Obesity in an older dog compounds the health problems that already accompany old age.

As your dog gets older, few of his organs function up to par. The kidneys slow down and the intestines become less efficient. These age-related factors are best handled with a change in diet and a change in feeding schedule to

FEEDING TIPS

Dog food must be at room temperature, neither too hot nor too cold. Fresh water, changed daily and served in a clean bowl, is mandatory, especially when feeding dried food.

Never feed your dog from the table while you are eating. Never feed your dog left-overs from your own meal. They usually contain too much fat and too much seasoning.

Dogs must chew their food. Hard pellets are excellent; soups and slurries are to be avoided.

Don't add left-overs or any extras to normal dog food. The normal food is usually balanced and adding something extra destroys the balance.

Except for age-related changes, dogs do not require dietary variations. They can be fed the same diet, day after day, without their becoming ill.

'DOES THIS COLLAR MAKE ME LOOK FAT?'

While humans may obsess about how they look and how trim their bodies are, many people believe that extra weight on their dogs is a good thing. The truth is, pets should not be over- or under-weight, as both can lead to or signal sickness. In order to tell how fit your pet is, run your hands over his ribs. Are his ribs buried under a layer of fat or are they sticking out consider-ably? If your pet is within his normal weight range, you should be able to feel the ribs easily. If you stand above him, the outline of his body should resemble an hourglass. Some breeds do tend to be leaner while some are a bit stockier, but making sure your dog is the right weight for his breed will certainly contribute to his good health.

DO DOGS HAVE TASTE BUDS?

Watching a dog 'wolf' or gobble his food, seemingly without chewing, leads an owner to wonder whether their dogs can taste anything. Yes, dogs have taste buds, with sensory perception of sweet, salty and sour. Puppies are born with fully mature taste buds.

give smaller portions that are more easily digested.

There is no single best diet for every older dog. While many dogs do well on light or senior diets, other dogs do better on puppy diets or other special premium diets such as lamb and rice. Be sensitive to your senior Berner's diet and this will help control other problems that may arise with your old friend.

WATER

Just as your dog needs proper nutrition from his food, water is an essential 'nutrient' as well. Water keeps the dog's body properly hydrated and promotes normal function of the body's systems. During house-training it is necessary to keep an eye on how much water your Bernese is drinking, but once he is reliably trained he should have access to clean fresh water at all times, especially if you feed dried food. Make certain that the dog's water bowl is clean, and change the water often.

DRINK, DRANK, DRUNK— MAKE IT A DOUBLE

In both humans and dogs, as well as most living organisms, water forms the major part of nearly every body tissue. Naturally, we take water for granted, but without it, life as we know it would cease.

For dogs, water is needed to keep their bodies functioning biochemically. Additionally, water is needed to replace the water lost while panting. Unlike humans who are able to sweat to dissipate heat, dogs must pant to cool down, thereby losing the vital water from their bodies needed to regulate their body temperatures. Humans lose electrolyte-containing products and other body-fluid components through sweating; dogs do not lose anything except water.

Water is essential always, but especially so when the weather is hot or humid or when your dog is exercising or working vigorously.

Experts recommend feeding the Berner from a bowl stand to help ward off bloat, which could result from the dog's craning its neck while eating.

EXERCISE

Working breeds require more exercise than most other breeds, and the Bernese Mountain Dog is

QUALITY FOOD

The cost of food must also be mentioned. All dogs need a good quality food with an adequate supply of protein to develop their bones and muscles properly. Most dogs are not picky eaters but unless fed properly can quickly succumb to skin problems.

no exception. A sedentary lifestyle is as harmful to a dog as it is to a person. The Bernese, a large dog with a substantial frame, needs to be walked twice daily for considerable distances. Berner pups should not be given vigorous exercise during the first year of life. Adults need free-running time as well to keep themselves fit. If you live in a home without a large fenced garden, you will have to commit to walking the dog for a

WHAT ARE YOU FEEDING YOUR DOG?

Read the label on your dog food. Many dog foods only advise what 50–55% of the contents are, leaving the other 45% in doubt.

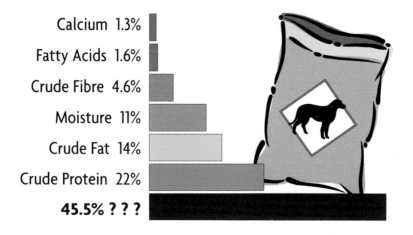

Calcium 1.3%
Fatty Acids 1.6%
Crude Fibre 4.6%
Moisture 11%
Crude Fat 14%
Crude Protein 22%
45.5% ? ? ?

few miles each day. For those who are more ambitious, you will find that your Bernese also enjoys an occasional hike, games of fetch or even a swim!

Bear in mind that an overweight dog should never be suddenly over-exercised; instead he should be encouraged to increase exercise slowly. Not only is exercise essential to keep the dog's body fit, it is essential to his mental well-being. A bored dog will find something to do, which often manifests itself in some type of destructive behaviour. In this sense, exercise is essential for the owner's mental well-being as well!

GROOMING

The Berner's coat is healthiest if brushed on a weekly basis. Regular frequent grooming is very beneficial to the dog's skin as well as the coat, as brushing massages the skin and distributes the natural oils throughout the coat, while also dispensing dirt and dust. Grooming a Bernese is not complicated or difficult. Basic tools include a coarse steel comb, a flea comb with closely spaced teeth and a slicker brush.

Start by brushing the long outer coat with the metal comb and loosen any snarls, then follow with your fine-toothed flea comb. Remove any loose hair with the slicker brush, brushing first against the grain, then with the

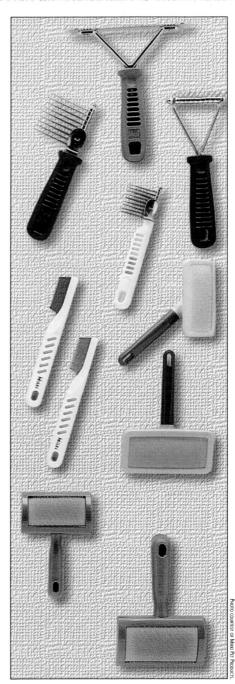

Your Berner's coat should be brushed on a regular basis. Your local pet shop will have an adequate supply of grooming tools from which you can select those tools most appropriate for the task.

PHOTO COURTESY OF MIKKI PET PRODUCTS.

grain for sheen. A damp chamois cloth is also handy for removing loose hair and dust.

Grooming, of course, also involves tending to the ears, eyes, teeth, feet and nails. A thorough body examination during grooming will disclose any lumps, sores or minor injuries or problems that may be hidden under the dense coat.

A well-kept Bernese should not require frequent bathing unless he gets into something smelly. Monthly baths are recommended, and a dry or waterless shampoo will spot-clean problem areas in between. Most Bernese moult about twice a year, and during those periods more frequent, even

GROOMING EQUIPMENT

How much grooming equipment you purchase will depend on how much grooming you are going to do. Here are some basics:

- Flea comb
- Chamois cloth
- Rake
- Slicker brush
- Metal comb
- Scissors
- Blaster
- Rubber mat
- Dog shampoo
- Spray hose attachment
- Ear cleaner
- Cotton wipes
- Towels
- Nail clippers

SOAP IT UP

The use of human soap products like shampoo, bubble bath and hand soap can be damaging to a dog's coat and skin. Human products are too strong and remove the protective oils coating the dog's hair and skin (that make him water-resistant). Use only shampoo made especially for dogs and you may like to use a medicated shampoo, which will always help to keep external parasites at bay.

daily, brushing, will keep dog hair around the home to a minimum. Frequent bathing during moulting season will also help speed up the shedding process.

BATHING

Like most anything, if you accustom your Berner to being bathed as a puppy, it will be second nature by the time he grows up. You want your dog to be at ease in the bath or else it could end up a wet, soapy, messy ordeal for both of you!

Brush your Bernese thoroughly before wetting his coat. This will get rid of most mats and tangles, which are harder to remove when the coat is wet. Make certain that your dog has a good non-slip surface to stand on. Begin by wetting the dog's coat. A shower or hose attachment is necessary for thoroughly wetting and rinsing the coat. Check the water temperature to make sure that it is neither too hot nor too cold.

Next, apply shampoo to the dog's coat and work it into a good lather. You should purchase a shampoo that is made for dogs. Do not use a product made for human hair. Wash the head last; you do not want shampoo to drip into the dog's eyes while you are washing the rest of his body. Work the shampoo all the way down to the skin. You can use this opportunity to check the skin for any bumps, bites or other abnormalities. Do not neglect any area of the body—get all of the hard-to-reach places.

Once the dog has been thoroughly shampooed, he requires an equally thorough

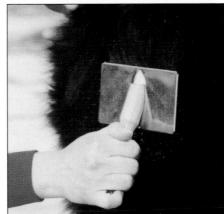

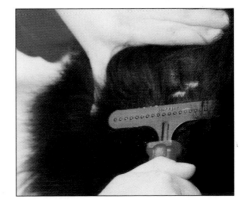

The Berner is a double-coated dog that will cast its coat twice per year, pushing out its soft undercoat. Purchase a top-quality rake or slicker brush to help remove the dead undercoat during grooming sessions.

BATHING BEAUTY

Once you are sure that the dog is thoroughly rinsed, squeeze the excess water out of the coat with your hand and dry him with a heavy towel. You may choose to use a blaster on his coat or just let it dry naturally. In cold weather, never allow your dog outside with a wet coat.

There are 'dry bath' products on the market, which are sprays and powders intended for spot cleaning, that can be used between regular baths, if necessary. They are not substitutes for regular baths, but they are easy to use for touch-ups as they do not require rinsing.

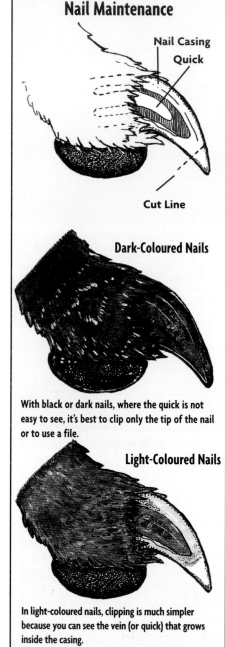

Nail Maintenance

Nail Casing

Quick

Cut Line

Dark-Coloured Nails

With black or dark nails, where the quick is not easy to see, it's best to clip only the tip of the nail or to use a file.

Light-Coloured Nails

In light-coloured nails, clipping is much simpler because you can see the vein (or quick) that grows inside the casing.

Your Berner's ears should be cleaned as frequently as your dog is groomed. Use soft cotton wipes with ear powder made especially for dogs.

rinsing. Shampoo left in the coat can be irritating to the skin. Protect his eyes from the shampoo by shielding them with your hand and directing the flow of water in the opposite direction. You should also avoid getting water in the ear canal. Be prepared for your dog to shake out his coat— you might want to stand back, but make sure you have a hold on the dog to keep him from running through the house.

EAR CLEANING

The ears should be kept clean with a cotton wipe and ear powder made especially for dogs. Be on the lookout for any signs of infection or ear mite infestation. If your Bernese has been shaking his head or scratching at his ears frequently, this usually indicates a problem. If his ears have an unusual odour, this is a sure sign of mite infestation or infection, and a signal to have his ears checked by the veterinary surgeon.

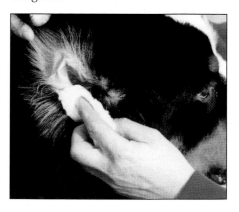

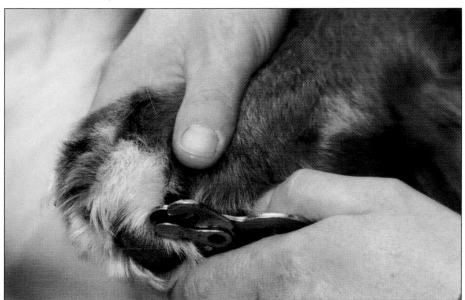

Your local pet shop sells nail clippers especially designed for dogs. Take instruction in how to use them. Start clipping your Berner's nails when the puppy is still young.

NAIL CLIPPING

Your Bernese should be accustomed to having his nails trimmed at an early age, since it will be part of your maintenance routine throughout his life. Not only does it look nicer, but long nails can scratch someone unintentionally. Also, a long nail has a better chance of ripping and bleeding, or causing the feet to spread. A good rule of thumb is that if you can hear your dog's nails clicking on the floor when he walks, his nails are too long.

Before you start cutting, make sure you can identify the 'quick' in each nail. The quick is a blood vessel that runs through the centre of each nail and grows rather close to the end. It will bleed if accidentally cut, which will be quite painful for the dog as it contains nerve endings. Keep some type of clotting agent on hand, such as a styptic pencil or styptic powder (the type used for shaving). This will stop the bleeding quickly when applied to the end of the cut nail. Do not panic if you cut the quick, just stop the bleeding and talk soothingly to your dog. Once he has calmed down, move on to the next nail. It is better to clip a little at a time, particularly with black-nailed dogs.

Hold your pup steady as you begin trimming his nails; you do not want him to make any sudden movements or run away. Talk to him soothingly and stroke him as you clip. Holding his foot in your hand, simply take off the end of each nail in one quick clip. You can purchase nail clippers that are specially made for dogs; you can probably find them wherever you buy pet or grooming supplies.

TRAVELLING WITH YOUR DOG

CAR TRAVEL

You should accustom your Bernese to riding in a car at an early age. You may or may not take him in the car often, but at the very least he will need to go to the vet and you do not want these trips to be traumatic for the dog or troublesome for you. The safest way for a dog to ride in the car is in his crate. If he uses a crate in the house, you can use the same crate for travel, provided your vehicle can accommodate such a large crate.

Put the pup in the crate and see how he reacts. If he seems uneasy, you can have a passenger hold him on his lap while you drive. Another option is a specially made safety harness for dogs, which straps the dog in much like a seat belt. Do not let the dog roam loose in the vehicle—this is very dangerous! If you should stop short, your dog can be thrown and injured. If the dog starts climbing on you and pestering you while you are driving, you will not be able to concentrate on the road. It is an unsafe situation for everyone— human and canine.

For long trips, be prepared to

The only safe way to travel with a Berner in the car or van is in his crate or behind a divider, which keeps the dog from disturbing the driver (and other passengers) while travelling.

stop to let the dog relieve himself. Take with you whatever you need to clean up after him, including some paper kitchen towels and perhaps some old towelling for use should he have an accident in the car or suffer from travel sickness.

AIR TRAVEL

While it is possible to take a dog on a flight within Britain, this is fairly unusual and advance permission is always required. The dog will be required to travel in a fibreglass crate and you should always check in advance with the airline regarding specific requirements. To help the dog be at ease, put one of his favourite toys in the crate with him. Do not feed the dog for at least six hours before the trip to minimise his need to relieve himself. However, certain regulations specify that water must always be made available to the dog in the crate.

Make sure your dog is properly identified and that your contact information appears on his ID tags and on his crate. Animals travel in a different area of the plane than human passengers, so every rule must be strictly followed so as to prevent the risk of getting separated from your dog.

BOARDING

So you want to take a family holiday—and you want to include

ON THE ROAD

If you are going on a long motor trip with your dog, be sure the hotels are dog friendly. Many hotels do not accept dogs. Also take along some ice that can be thawed and offered to your dog if he becomes overheated. Most dogs like to lick ice.

all members of the family. You would probably make arrangements for accommodation ahead of time anyway, but this is especially important when travelling with a dog. You do not want to make an overnight stop at the only place around for miles and find out that they do not allow dogs. Also, you do not want to reserve a place for your family without confirming that you are travelling with a dog because, if it is against their policy, you may not have a place to stay.

Alternatively, if you are travelling and choose not to bring your Bernese, you will have to make arrangements for him while you are away. Some options are to take him to a neighbour's house to stay while you are gone, to have a trusted neighbour pop in often or stay at your house or to bring your dog to a reputable boarding kennel. If you choose to board him at a kennel, you should visit in advance to see the facilities provided, how clean they are and

If you acquire your Berner from a local breeder, you might be fortunate enough to board the dog with the breeder when you are on holiday. Otherwise, you will have to seek out a reputable facility near your home.

where the dogs are kept. Talk to some of the employees and see how they treat the dogs—do they spend time with the dogs, play with them, exercise them, etc.?

IDENTIFICATION OPTIONS

As puppies become more and more expensive, especially those puppies of high quality for showing and/or breeding, they have a greater chance of being stolen. The usual collar dog tag is, of course, easily removed. But there are two techniques that have become widely used for identification.

The puppy microchip implantation involves the injection of a small microchip, about the size of a corn kernel, under the skin of the dog. If your dog shows up at a clinic or shelter, or is offered for resale under less than savoury circumstances, it can be positively identified by the microchip. The microchip is scanned and a registry quickly identifies you as the owner. This is not only protection against theft, but should the dog run away or go chasing a squirrel and get lost, you have a fair chance of getting it back.

Tattooing is done on various parts of the dog, from its belly to its cheeks. The number tattooed can be your telephone number or any other number which you can easily memorise. When professional dog thieves see a tattooed dog, they usually lose interest in it. Both microchipping and tattooing can be done at your local veterinary clinic. For the safety of our dogs, no laboratory facility or dog broker will accept a tattooed dog as stock.

Your Berner should always wear his identification tag attached to his everyday collar.

Also find out the kennel's policy on vaccinations and what they require. This is for all of the dogs' safety, since when dogs are kept together, there is a greater risk of diseases being passed from dog to dog.

IDENTIFICATION

Your Berner is your valued companion and friend. That is why you always keep a close eye on him and you have made sure that he cannot escape from the garden or wriggle out of his collar and run away from you. However, accidents can happen and there may come a time when your dog unexpectedly gets separated from you. If this unfortunate event should occur, the first thing on your mind will be finding him. Proper identification, including an ID tag as well as a tattoo and/or a microchip, will increase the chances of his being returned to you safely and quickly.

TATTOOING

In Switzerland all puppies must be tattooed with their future registration number on their ear flaps at about six weeks of age.

REAP THE REWARDS

If you start with a normal, healthy dog and give him time, patience and some carefully executed lessons, you will reap the rewards of that training for the life of the dog. And what a life it will be! The two of you will find immeasurable pleasure in the companionship you have built together with love, respect and understanding.

Living with an untrained dog is a lot like owning a piano that you do not know how to play—it is a nice object to look at but it does not do much more than that to bring you pleasure. Now try taking piano lessons and suddenly the piano comes alive and brings forth magical sounds and rhythms that set your heart singing and your body swaying.

The same is true with your Bernese Mountain Dog. Any dog is a big responsibility and if not trained sensibly may develop unacceptable behaviour that annoys you or could even cause family friction.

To train your Berner, you may like to enrol in an obedience class. Teach him good manners as you learn how and why he behaves the way he does. Find out how to communicate with your dog and how to recognise and understand his communications with you. Suddenly the dog takes on a new role in your life—he is clever, interesting, well-behaved and fun to be with. He demonstrates his bond of devotion to you daily. In other words, your

Bernese does wonders for your ego because he constantly reminds you that you are not only his leader, you are his hero!

Those involved with teaching dog obedience and counselling owners about their dogs' behaviour have discovered some interesting facts about dog ownership. For example, training dogs when they are puppies results in the highest rate of success in developing well-mannered and well-adjusted adult dogs. Training an older dog, from six months to six years of age, can produce almost equal results providing that the owner accepts the dog's slower rate of learning capability and is willing to work patiently to help the dog succeed at developing to his fullest potential. Unfortunately, many owners of untrained adult dogs lack the patience factor, so they do not persist until their dogs are successful at learning particular behaviours.

Training a puppy aged 10 to 16 weeks (20 weeks at the most) is like working with a dry sponge in a pool of water. The pup soaks up

THE HAND THAT FEEDS

To a dog's way of thinking, your hands are like his mouth in terms of a defence mechanism. If you squeeze him too tightly, he might just bite you because that would be his normal response. This is not aggressive biting and, although all biting should be discouraged, you need the discipline in learning how to handle your dog.

whatever you show him and constantly looks for more things to do and learn. At this early age, his body is not yet producing hormones, and therein lies the reason for such a high rate of success. Without hormones, he is focused on his owners and not particularly interested in investigating other places, dogs, people,

OPEN MINDS

Dogs are as different from each other as people are. What works for one dog may not work for another. Have an open mind. If one method of training is unsuccessful, try another.

Teaching a puppy right from wrong is easier when the puppy is less than 20 weeks old, and easiest when you catch the pup in the act of wrongdoing.

etc. You are his leader: his provider of food, water, shelter and security. He latches onto you and wants to stay close. He will usually follow you from room to room, will not let you out of his sight when you are outdoors with him and will respond in like manner to the people and animals you encounter. If you greet a friend warmly, he will be happy to greet the person as well. If, however, you are hesitant, even anxious, about the approach of a

THINK BEFORE YOU BARK
Dogs are sensitive to their master's moods and emotions. Use your voice wisely when communicating with your dog. Never raise your voice at your dog unless you are trying to correct him. 'Barking' at your dog can become as meaningless as 'dogspeak' is to you. Think before you bark!

stranger, he will respond accordingly.

Once the puppy begins to produce hormones, his natural curiosity emerges and he begins to investigate the world around him. It is at this time when you may notice that the untrained dog begins to wander away from you and even ignore your commands to stay close. When this behaviour becomes a problem, the owner has

TRAINING TIP
Dogs will do anything for your attention. If you reward the dog when he is calm and resting, you will develop a well-mannered dog. If, on the other hand, you greet your dog excitedly and encourage him to wrestle with you, the dog will greet you the same way and you will have a hyperactive dog on your hands.

two choices: get rid of the dog or train him. It is strongly urged that you choose the latter option.

There are usually classes within a reasonable distance from the owner's home, but you can also do a lot to train your dog yourself. Sometimes there are classes available but the tuition is too costly. Whatever the circumstances, the solution to the problem of lack of lesson availability lies within the pages of this book.

This chapter is devoted to

HONOUR AND OBEY
Dogs are the most honourable animals in existence. They consider another species (humans) as their own. They interface with you. You are their leader. Puppies perceive children to be on their level; their actions around small children are different from their behaviour around their adult masters.

helping you train your Berner at home. If the recommended procedures are followed faithfully, you may expect positive results that will prove rewarding both to you and your dog.

Whether your new charge is a puppy or a mature adult, the methods of teaching and the techniques we use in training basic behaviours are the same. After all, no dog, whether puppy or adult, likes harsh or inhumane methods. All creatures, however, respond favourably to gentle motivational methods and sincere praise and encouragement. Now let us get started.

TOILET-TRAINING

You can train a puppy to relieve itself wherever you choose, but this must be somewhere suitable. You should bear in mind from the outset that when your puppy is old enough to go out in public places, any canine deposits must

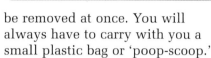

TAKE THE LEAD

Do not carry your dog to his toilet area. Lead him there on a leash or, better yet, encourage him to follow you to the spot. If you start carrying him to his spot, you might end up doing this routine forever and your dog will have the satisfaction of having trained YOU.

be removed at once. You will always have to carry with you a small plastic bag or 'poop-scoop.'

Outdoor training includes such surfaces as grass, soil and cement. Indoor training usually means training your dog to newspaper.

When deciding on the surface and location that you will want your Bernese to use, be sure it is going to be permanent. Training

MEALTIME

Mealtime should be a peaceful time for your puppy. Do not put his food and water bowls in a high-traffic area in the house. For example, give him his own little corner of the kitchen where he can eat undisturbed and where he will not be underfoot. Do not allow small children or other family members to disturb the pup when he is eating.

Toilet training, anyone? Remember what goes in must come out, so keep the amount of water your Berner puppy drinks in mind during house-training.

CANINE DEVELOPMENT SCHEDULE

It is important to understand how and at what age a puppy develops into adulthood. If you are a puppy owner, consult the following Canine Development Schedule to determine the stage of development your puppy is currently experiencing. This knowledge will help you as you work with the puppy in the weeks and months ahead.

Period	Age	Characteristics
FIRST TO THIRD	BIRTH TO SEVEN WEEKS	Puppy needs food, sleep and warmth, and responds to simple and gentle touching. Needs mother for security and disciplining. Needs littermates for learning and interacting with other dogs. Pup learns to function within a pack and learns pack order of dominance. Begin socialising with adults and children for short periods. Begins to become aware of its environment.
FOURTH	EIGHT TO TWELVE WEEKS	Brain is fully developed. Needs socialising with outside world. Remove from mother and littermates. Needs to change from canine pack to human pack. Human dominance necessary. Fear period occurs between 8 and 12 weeks. Avoid fright and pain.
FIFTH	THIRTEEN TO SIXTEEN WEEKS	Training and formal obedience should begin. Less association with other dogs, more with people, places, situations. Period will pass easily if you remember this is pup's change-to-adolescence time. Be firm and fair. Flight instinct prominent. Permissiveness and over-disciplining can do permanent damage. Praise for good behaviour.
JUVENILE	FOUR TO EIGHT MONTHS	Another fear period about 7 to 8 months of age. It passes quickly, but be cautious of fright and pain. Sexual maturity reached. Dominant traits established. Dog should understand sit, down, come and stay by now.

NOTE: THESE ARE APPROXIMATE TIME FRAMES. ALLOW FOR INDIVIDUAL DIFFERENCES IN PUPPIES.

your dog to grass and then changing your mind two months later is extremely difficult for both dog and owner.

Next, choose the command you will use each and every time you want your puppy to void. 'Hurry up' and 'Toilet' are examples of commands commonly used by dog owners.

Get in the habit of giving the puppy your chosen relief command before you take him out. That way, when he becomes an adult, you will be able to determine if he wants to go out when you ask him. A confirmation will be signs of interest, wagging his tail, watching you intently, going to the door, etc.

PUPPY'S NEEDS

Puppy needs to relieve himself after play periods, after each meal, after he has been sleeping and at any time he indicates that he is looking for a place to urinate or defecate.

The urinary and intestinal tract muscles of very young puppies are not fully developed. Therefore, like human babies,

> **ATTENTION!**
> Your dog is actually training you at the same time you are training him. Dogs do things to get attention. They usually repeat whatever succeeds in getting your attention.

> **PAPER CAPER**
> Never line your pup's sleeping area with newspaper. Puppy litters are usually raised on newspaper and, once in your home, the puppy will immediately associate newspaper with voiding. Never put newspaper on any floor while house-training, as this will only confuse the puppy. If you are paper-training him, use paper in his designated relief area ONLY. Finally, restrict water intake after evening meals. Offer a few licks at a time—never let a young puppy gulp water after meals.

puppies need to relieve themselves frequently.

Take your puppy out often—every hour for an eight-week-old, for example, and always immediately

Your puppy will welcome his crate as his own special place in no time. The crate is the best toilet-training method for Berners, and more and more breeders are recommending crates for reinforcing house-training.

after sleeping and eating. The older the puppy, the less often he will need to relieve himself. Finally, as a mature healthy adult, he will require only three to five relief trips per day.

HOUSING

Since the types of housing and control you provide for your puppy have a direct relationship on the success of house-training, we consider the various aspects of both before we begin training.

Taking a new puppy home and turning him loose in your house can be compared to turning a child loose in a sports arena and telling the child that the place is all his! The sheer enormity of the place would be too much for him to handle.

Instead, offer the puppy clearly defined areas where he can play, sleep, eat and live. A room of the house where the family gathers is the most obvious choice. Puppies are social animals and need to feel a part of the pack right from the start. Hearing your voice, watching you while you are doing things and smelling you nearby are all positive reinforcers that he is now a member of your pack. Usually a family room, the kitchen or a nearby adjoining breakfast area is ideal for providing safety and security for both puppy and owner.

Within that room there should be a smaller area that the puppy can call his own. An alcove, a wire or fibreglass dog crate or a fenced (not boarded!) corner from which he can view the activities of his new family will be fine. The size of the area or crate is the key factor here. The area must be large enough for the puppy to lie down and stretch out as well as stand up without rubbing his head on the top, yet small enough so that he cannot relieve himself at one end and sleep at the other without coming into contact with his droppings until fully trained to relieve himself outside.

Dogs are, by nature, clean animals and will not remain close to their relief areas unless forced to do so. In those cases, they then become dirty dogs and usually remain that way for life.

The designated area should contain clean bedding and a toy. Water must always be available, in a non-spill container.

CONTROL

By control, we mean helping the puppy to create a lifestyle pattern that will be compatible to that of his human pack (YOU!). Just as we guide little children to learn our way of life, we must show the puppy when it is time to play, eat, sleep, exercise and even entertain himself.

Your puppy should always sleep in his crate. He should also learn that, during times of household confusion and

PARENTAL GUIDANCE

Training a dog is a life experience. Many parents admit that much of what they know about raising children they learned from caring for their dogs. Dogs respond to love, fairness and guidance, just as children do. Become a good dog owner and you may become an even better parent.

excessive human activity such as at breakfast when family members are preparing for the day, he can play by himself in relative safety and comfort in his designated area. Each time you leave the puppy alone, he should understand exactly where he is to stay. Puppies are chewers. They cannot tell the difference between lamp cords, television wires, shoes, table legs, etc. Chewing into a television wire, for example, can be fatal to the puppy while a shorted wire can start a fire in the house.

If the puppy chews on the arm of the chair when he is alone, you will probably discipline him angrily when you get home. Thus, he makes the association that your coming home means he is going to be punished. (He will not remember chewing the chair and is incapable of making the association of the discipline with his naughty deed.)

Other times of excitement, such as family parties, etc., can be fun for the puppy providing he can view the activities from the security of his designated area. He is not underfoot and he is not being fed all sorts of titbits that will probably cause him stomach distress, yet he still feels a part of the fun.

SCHEDULE

A puppy should be taken to his relief area each time he is released from his designated area, after meals, after a play session and when he first awakens in the morning (at age eight weeks, this can mean 5 a.m.!). The puppy will indicate that he's ready 'to go' by circling or sniffing busily—do not misinterpret these signs. For a puppy less than ten weeks of age, a routine of taking him out every

Never underestimate the power of the canine nose. Puppies remember every microcosm of scent, which can complicate house-training if you do not properly sanitise the area after an accident.

hour is necessary. As the puppy grows, he will be able to wait for longer periods of time.

Keep trips to his relief area short. Stay no more than five or six minutes and then return to the house. If he goes during that time, praise him lavishly and take him indoors immediately. If he does not, but he has an accident when you go back indoors, pick him up immediately, say 'No! No!' and return to his relief area. Wait a few minutes, then return to the house again. Never hit a puppy or rub

THE SUCCESS METHOD

Success that comes by luck is usually short lived. Success that comes by well-thought-out proven methods is often more easily achieved and permanent. This is the Success Method. It is designed to give you, the puppy owner, a simple yet proven way to help your puppy develop clean living habits and a feeling of security in his new environment.

THE SUCCESS METHOD

1 Tell the puppy 'Crate time!' and place him in the crate with a small treat (a piece of cheese or half of a biscuit). Let him stay in the crate for five minutes while you are in the same room. Then release him and praise lavishly. Never release him when he is fussing. Wait until he is quiet before you let him out.

2 Repeat Step 1 several times a day.

3 The next day, place the puppy in the crate as before. Let him stay there for ten minutes. Do this several times.

4 Continue building time in five-minute increments until the puppy

stays in his crate for 30 minutes with you in the room. Always take him to his relief area after prolonged periods in his crate.

5 Now go back to Step 1 and let the puppy stay in his crate for five minutes, this time while you are out of the room.

6 Once again, build crate time in five-minute increments with you out of the room. When the puppy will stay willingly in his crate (he may even fall asleep!) for 30 minutes with you out of the room, he will be ready to stay in it for several hours at a time.

6 Steps to Successful Crate Training

HOW MANY TIMES A DAY?

AGE	RELIEF TRIPS
To 14 weeks	10
14–22 weeks	8
22–32 weeks	6
Adulthood	4
(dog stops growing)	

These are estimates, of course, but they are a guide to the MINIMUM opportunities a dog should have each day to relieve itself.

Always clean up after your Berner has relieved itself, whether it is in a public place or in your own garden.

his face in urine or excrement when he has had an accident!

Once indoors, put the puppy in his crate until you have had time to clean up his accident. Then release him to the family area and watch him more closely than before. Chances are, his accident was a result of your not picking up his signal or waiting too long before offering him the opportunity to relieve himself. Never hold a grudge against the puppy for accidents.

THE CLEAN LIFE

By providing sleeping and resting quarters that fit the dog, and offering frequent opportunities to relieve himself outside his quarters, the puppy quickly learns that the outdoors (or the newspaper if you are training him to paper) is the place to go when he needs to urinate or defecate. It also reinforces his innate desire to keep his sleeping quarters clean. This, in turn, helps develop the muscle control that will eventually produce a dog with clean living habits.

'NO' MEANS 'NO!'

Dogs do not understand our language. They can be trained to react to a certain sound, at a certain volume. If you say 'No, Oliver' in a very soft pleasant voice it will not have the same meaning as 'No, Oliver!!' when you shout it as loud as you can. You should never use the dog's name during a reprimand, just the command NO!! Since dogs don't understand words, comics often use dogs trained with opposite meanings. Thus, when the comic commands his dog to SIT the dog will stand up, and vice versa.

Be fair and consistent when training your Berner. Few breeds are as sensitive to human emotions.

Let the puppy learn that going outdoors means it is time to relieve himself, not play. Once trained, he will be able to play indoors and out and still differen-tiate between the times for play versus the times for relief.

Help him develop regular hours for naps, being alone, playing by himself and just resting, all in his crate. Encourage him to entertain himself while you are busy with your activities. Let him learn that having you near is comforting, but it is not your main purpose in life to provide him with undivided attention.

Each time you put a puppy in his own area, use the same command, whatever suits best. Soon he will run to his crate or special area when he hears you say those words.

Crate training provides safety for you, the puppy and the home. It also provides the puppy with a feeling of security, and that helps the puppy achieve self-confidence and clean habits.

Remember that one of the primary ingredients in house-training your puppy is control. Regardless of your lifestyle, there will always be occasions when you will need to have a place where your dog can stay and be happy and safe. Crate training is the answer for now and in the future.

In conclusion, a few key elements are really all you need for a successful house-training method—consistency, frequency, praise, control and supervision. By following these procedures with a normal, healthy puppy, you and the puppy will soon be past the stage of 'accidents' and ready to move on to a full and rewarding life together.

ROLES OF DISCIPLINE, REWARD AND PUNISHMENT

Discipline, training one to act in accordance with rules, brings order to life. It is as simple as that. Without discipline, particularly in a group society, chaos reigns supreme and the group will eventually perish. Humans and canines are social animals and need some form of discipline in order to function effectively. They must procure food, protect their home base and their young and reproduce to keep the species going.

If there were no discipline in the lives of social animals, they would eventually die from starvation and/or predation by other stronger animals.

In the case of domestic canines, dogs need discipline in their lives in order to understand how their pack (you and other family members) functions and how they must act in order to survive.

A large humane society in a highly populated area recently surveyed dog owners regarding their satisfaction with their relationships with their dogs. People who had trained their dogs were 75% more satisfied with

KEEP SMILING
Never train your dog, puppy or adult, when you are angry or in a sour mood. Dogs are very sensitive to human feelings, especially anger, and if your dog senses that you are angry or upset, he will connect your anger with his training and learn to resent or fear his training sessions.

their pets than those who had never trained their dogs.

Dr Edward Thorndike, a psychologist, established *Thorndike's Theory of Learning*, which states that a behaviour that results in a pleasant event tends to be repeated. A behaviour that results in an unpleasant event tends not to be repeated. It is this theory on which training methods

outside source. For example, a child is told not to touch the stove because he may get burned. He disobeys and touches the stove. In doing so, he receives a burn. From that time on, he respects the heat of the stove and avoids contact with it. Therefore, a behaviour that results in an unpleasant event tends not to be repeated.

A good example of a dog learning the hard way is the dog who chases the house cat. He is told many times to leave the cat alone, yet he persists in teasing the cat. Then, one day he begins chasing the cat but the cat turns and swipes a claw across the dog's face, leaving him with a painful gash on his nose. The final result is that the dog stops chasing the cat.

TRAINING EQUIPMENT

COLLAR AND LEAD
For a Bernese Mountain Dog, the collar and lead that you use for training must be one with which you are easily able to work, not too heavy for the dog and perfectly safe.

TREATS
Have a bag of treats on hand. Something nutritious and easy to swallow works best. Use a soft treat, a chunk of cheese or a piece of cooked chicken rather than a dry biscuit. By the time the dog has finished chewing a dry treat,

are based today. For example, if you manipulate a dog to perform a specific behaviour and reward him for doing it, he is likely to do it again because he enjoyed the end result.

Occasionally, punishment, a penalty inflicted for an offence, is necessary. The best type of punishment often comes from an

Discourage your puppy from chewing on his lead or it will become a difficult habit to break.

he will forget why he is being rewarded in the first place! Using food rewards will not teach a dog to beg at the table—the only way to teach a dog to beg at the table is to give him food from the table. In training, rewarding the dog with a food treat will help him associate praise and the treats with learning new behaviours that obviously please his owner.

TRAINING BEGINS: ASK THE DOG A QUESTION

In order to teach your Berner anything, you must first get his attention. After all, he cannot learn anything if he is looking away from you with his mind on something else.

To get his attention, ask him, 'School?' and immediately walk over to him and give him a treat as you tell him 'Good dog.' Wait a minute or two and repeat the routine, this time with a treat in your hand as you approach within a foot of the dog. Do not go directly to him, but stop about a foot short of him and hold out the treat as you ask, 'School?' He will see you approaching with a treat in your hand and most likely begin walking toward you. As you meet, give him the treat and praise again.

The third time, ask the question, have a treat in your hand and walk only a short distance toward the dog so that he must walk almost all the way to

TRAINING RULES

If you want to be successful in training your dog, you have four rules to obey yourself:

1. Develop an understanding of how a dog thinks.
2. Do not blame the dog for lack of communication.
3. Define your dog's personality and act accordingly.
4. Have patience and be consistent.

you. As he reaches you, give him the treat and praise again.

By this time, the dog will probably be getting the idea that if he pays attention to you, especially when you ask that question, it will pay off in treats and enjoyable activities for him. In other words, he learns that 'school' means doing great things

Teaching sit to
a stubborn
Berner may
require a little
presure on the
dog's rear
quarters.

COMMAND STANCE

Stand up straight and
authoritatively when giving your
dog commands. Do not issue
commands when lying on the
floor or lying on your back on the
sofa. If you are on your hands and
knees when you give a command,
your dog will think you are
positioning yourself to play.

with you that are fun and result in
positive attention for him.

Remember that the dog does
not understand your verbal
language; he only recognises
sounds. Your question translates
to a series of sounds for him, and
those sounds become the signal
to go to you and pay attention; if
he does, he will get to interact
with you plus receive treats and
praise.

THE BASIC COMMANDS

TEACHING SIT

Now that you have the dog's
attention, attach his lead and
hold it in your left hand and a
food treat in your right. Place
your food hand at the dog's nose
and let him lick the treat but not
take it from you. Say 'Sit' and
slowly raise your food hand from
in front of the dog's nose up over
his head so that he is looking at
the ceiling. As he bends his head
upward, he will have to bend his
knees to maintain his balance. As
he bends his knees, he will
assume a sit position. At that
point, release the food treat and
praise lavishly with comments
such as 'Good dog! Good sit!,'
etc. Remember to always praise
enthusiastically, because dogs
relish verbal praise from their
owners and feel so proud of
themselves whenever they
accomplish a behaviour.

You will not use food forever
in getting the dog to obey your
commands. Food is only used to
teach new behaviours, and once
the dog knows what you want
when you give a specific
command, you will wean him off
the food treats but still maintain
the verbal praise. After all, you
will always have your voice with
you, and there will be many
times when you have no food
rewards but expect the dog to
obey.

TEACHING DOWN

Teaching the down exercise is easy when you understand how the dog perceives the down position, and it is very difficult when you do not. Dogs perceive the down position as a submissive one, therefore teaching the down exercise using a forceful method can sometimes make the dog develop such a fear of the down that he either runs away when you say 'Down' or he attempts to snap at the person who tries to force him down.

Have the dog sit close alongside your left leg, facing in the same direction as you are. Hold the lead in your left hand and a food treat in your right. Now place your left hand lightly on the top of the dog's shoulders where they meet above the spinal cord. Do not push down on the dog's shoulders; simply rest your left hand there so you can guide the dog to lie down close to your left leg rather than to swing away from your side when he drops.

Now place the food hand at the dog's nose, say 'Down' very softly (almost a whisper), and slowly lower the food hand to the dog's front feet. When the food hand reaches the floor, begin moving it forward along the floor in front of the dog. Keep talking softly to the dog, saying things like, 'Do you want this treat? You can do this, good dog.' Your reassuring tone of voice will help calm the dog as he tries to follow the food hand in order to get the treat.

When the dog's elbows touch the floor, release the food and praise softly. Try to get the dog to maintain that down position for several seconds before you let him sit up again. The goal here is to get the dog to settle down and not feel threatened in the down position.

TEACHING STAY

It is easy to teach the dog to stay in either a sit or a down position.

DOUBLE JEOPARDY

A dog in jeopardy never lies down. He stays alert on his feet because instinct tells him that he may have to run away or fight for his survival. Therefore, if a dog feels threatened or anxious, he will not lie down. Consequently, it is important to have the dog calm and relaxed as he learns the down exercise.

CONSISTENCY PAYS OFF
Dogs need consistency in their feeding schedule, exercise and toilet breaks and in the verbal commands you use. If you use 'Stay' on Monday and 'Stay here, please' on Tuesday, you will confuse your dog. Don't demand perfect behaviour during training classes and then let him have the run of the house the rest of the day. Above all, lavish praise on your pet consistently every time he does something right. The more he feels he is pleasing you, the more willing he will be to learn.

Again, we use food and praise during the teaching process as we help the dog to understand exactly what it is that we are expecting him to do.

To teach the sit/stay, start with the dog sitting on your left side as before and hold the lead in your left hand. Have a food treat in your right hand and place your food hand at the dog's nose. Say 'Stay' and step out on your right foot to stand directly in front of the dog, toe to toe, as he licks and nibbles the treat. Be sure to keep his head facing upward to maintain the sit position. Count to five and then swing around to stand next to the dog again with him on your left. As soon as you get back to the original position, release the food and praise lavishly.

To teach the down/stay, do the down as previously described. As soon as the dog lies down, say 'Stay' and step out on your right foot just as you did in the sit/stay. Count to five and then return to stand beside the dog with him on your left side. Release the treat and praise as always.

Within a week or ten days, you can begin to add a bit of distance between you and your dog when you leave him. When you do, use your left hand open with the palm facing the dog as a stay signal, much the same as the hand signal a constable uses to stop traffic at an intersection. Hold the food treat in your right hand as before, but this time the food is not touching the dog's nose. He will watch the food hand and quickly learn that he is going to get that treat as soon as you return to his side.

When you can stand 1 metre away from your dog for 30 seconds, you can then begin building time and distance in both stays. Eventually, the dog can be expected to remain in the stay position for prolonged periods of time until you return to him or call him to you. Always praise lavishly when he stays.

TEACHING COME
If you make teaching 'come' an exciting experience, you should

never have a 'student' that does not love the game or that fails to come when called. The secret, it seems, is never to teach the word 'come.'

At times when an owner most wants his dog to come when called, the owner is likely to be upset or anxious and he allows these feelings to come through in the tone of his voice when he calls his dog. Hearing that desperation in his owner's voice, the dog fears the results of going to him and therefore either disobeys outright or runs in the opposite direction. The secret, therefore, is to teach the dog a game and, when you want him to come to you, simply play the game. It is practically a no-fail solution!

To begin, have several members of your family take a few food treats and each go into a different room in the house. Take turns calling the dog, and each person should celebrate the dog's finding him with a treat and lots

> ### 'COME' . . . BACK
> Never call your dog to come to you for a correction or scold him when he reaches you. That is the quickest way to turn a 'Come' command into 'Go away fast!' Dogs think only in the present tense, and your dog will connect the scolding with coming to you, not with the misbehaviour of a few moments earlier.

> ### 'WHERE ARE YOU?'
> When calling the dog, do not say 'Come.' Say things like, 'Rover, where are you? See if you can find me! I have a biscuit for you!' Keep up a constant line of chatter with coaxing sounds and frequent questions such as, 'Where are you?' The dog will learn to follow the sound of your voice to locate you and receive his reward.

of happy praise. When a person calls the dog, he is actually inviting the dog to find him and get a treat as a reward for 'winning.'

A few turns of the 'Where are you?' game and the dog will understand that everyone is playing the game and that each person has a big celebration awaiting his success at locating them. Once he learns to love the game, simply calling out 'Where are you?' will bring him running from wherever he is when he hears that all-important question.

The come command is recognised as one of the most important things to teach a dog, but there are trainers who work with thousands of dogs and never teach the actual word 'Come.' Yet these dogs will race to respond to a person who uses the dog's name followed by 'Where are you?' For example, a woman has a 12-year-

FAMILY TIES

If you have other pets in the home and/or interact often with the pets of friends and other family members, your pup will respond to those pets in much the same manner as you do. It is only when you show fear of or resentment toward another animal that he will act fearful or unfriendly.

The goal of heel training is to have your Berner walk beside you on lead without pulling. The rewards of a properly heel-trained dog are evident every time you take your dog for a peaceful, leisurely stroll.

old companion dog who went blind, but who never fails to locate her owner when asked, 'Where are you?'

Children, in particular, love to play this game with their dogs. Children can hide in smaller places like a shower or bath, behind a bed or under a table. The dog needs to work a little bit harder to find these hiding places, but when he does he loves to celebrate with a treat and a tussle with a favourite youngster.

TEACHING HEEL

Heeling means that the dog walks beside the owner without pulling. It takes time and patience on the

owner's part to succeed at teaching the dog that he (the owner) will not proceed unless the dog is walking calmly beside him. Pulling out ahead on the lead is definitely not acceptable.

Begin by holding the lead in your left hand as the dog sits beside your left leg. Move the loop end of the lead to your right hand but keep your left hand short on the lead so it keeps the dog in close next to you.

Say 'Heel' and step forward on your left foot. Keep the dog close to you and take three steps. Stop and have the dog sit next to you in what we now call the 'heel position.' Praise verbally, but do not touch the dog. Hesitate a moment and begin again with 'Heel,' taking three steps and stopping, at which point the dog is told to sit again.

Your goal here is to have the dog walk those three steps without pulling on the lead. Once he will walk calmly beside you

TUG OF WALK?

If you begin teaching the heel by taking long walks and letting the dog pull you along, he misinterprets this action as an acceptable form of taking a walk. When you pull back on the lead to counteract his pulling, he reads that tug as a signal to pull even harder!

for three steps without pulling, increase the number of steps you take to five. When he will walk politely beside you while you take five steps, you can increase the length of your walk to ten steps. Keep increasing the length of your stroll until the dog will walk quietly beside you without pulling as long as you want him to heel. When you stop heeling, indicate to the dog that the exercise is over by verbally praising as you pet him and say 'OK, good dog.' The 'OK' is used as a release word, meaning that the exercise is finished and the dog is free to relax.

If you are dealing with a dog who insists on pulling you around, simply 'put on your brakes' and stand your ground until the dog realises that the two of you are not going anywhere until he is beside you and moving at your pace, not his. It may take some time just standing there to convince the dog that you are the leader and you will be the one to

decide on the direction and speed of your travel.

Each time the dog looks up at you or slows down to give a slack lead between the two of you, quietly praise him and say, 'Good heel. Good dog.' Eventually, the dog will begin to respond and within a few days he will be walking politely beside you without pulling on the lead. At first, the training sessions should be kept short and very positive; soon the dog will be able to walk nicely with you for increasingly longer distances. Remember also

HEELING WELL

Teach your dog to HEEL in an enclosed area. Once you think the dog will obey reliably and you want to attempt advanced obedience exercises such as off-lead heeling, test him in a fenced-in area so he cannot run away.

to give the dog free time and the opportunity to run and play when you have finished heel practice.

WEANING OFF FOOD IN TRAINING

Food is used in training new behaviours. Once the dog understands what behaviour goes with a specific command, it is time to start weaning him off the food treats. At first, give a treat after each exercise. Then, start to give a treat only after every other exercise. Mix up the times when you offer a food reward and the times when you only offer praise so that the dog will never know when he is going to receive both food and praise and when he is going to receive only praise. This is called a variable ratio reward system and it proves successful because there is always the chance that the owner will produce a treat, so the dog never stops trying for that reward. No matter what, *always* give verbal praise.

OBEDIENCE CLASSES

It is a good idea to enrol in an obedience class if one is available in your area. If yours is a show dog, ringcraft classes would be more appropriate. Many areas have dog clubs that offer basic obedience training as well as preparatory classes for obedience competition. There are also local dog trainers who offer similar classes.

At dog shows, dogs can earn

> **PRACTICE MAKES PERFECT!**
> • Have training lessons with your dog every day in several short segments— three to five times a day for a few minutes at a time is ideal.
> • Do not have long practice sessions. The dog will become easily bored.
> • Never practise when you are tired, ill, worried or in an otherwise negative mood. This will transmit to the dog and may have an adverse effect on its performance.
> Think fun, short and above all POSITIVE! End each session on a high note, rather than a failed exercise, and make sure to give a lot of praise. Enjoy the training and help your dog enjoy it, too.

titles at various levels of competition. The beginning levels of competition include basic behaviours such as sit, down, heel, etc. The more advanced levels of competition include jumping, retrieving, scent discrimination and signal work. The advanced levels require a dog and owner to put a lot of time and effort into their training and the titles that can be earned at these levels of competition are very prestigious.

OTHER ACTIVITIES FOR LIFE

Whether a dog is trained in the structured environment of a class or alone with his owner at home, there are many activities that can bring fun and rewards to both owner and dog once they have mastered basic control.

Teaching the dog to help out around the home, in the garden or on the farm provides great satisfaction to both dog and owner. In addition, the dog's help makes life a little easier for his owner and raises his stature as a valued companion to his family. It helps give the dog a purpose by occupying his mind and providing an outlet for his energy.

Backpacking is another exciting and healthy activity that the dog can be taught without assistance from more than his owner. The exercise of walking and climbing is good for man and dog alike, and the bond that they develop together is priceless. The rule for backpacking with any dog is never to expect the dog to carry more than one-sixth of his body weight.

If you are interested in participating in organised competition with your Bernese, there are activities other than obedience in which you and your dog can become involved. Agility is a popular sport where dogs run through an obstacle course that includes various jumps, tunnels and other exercises to test the dog's speed and coordination. The owners run beside their dogs to give commands and to guide them through the course. Although competitive, the focus is on fun— it's fun to do, fun to watch and great exercise.

If a Bernese owner wants to take advantage of the breed's draughting ability, carting is the most popular mountain-dog activity. There are clubs that organise carting events, all of which are brilliant enjoyment for dog and owner, some of which are competitive with prizes.

FEAR AGGRESSION

Pups who are subjected to physical abuse during training commonly end up with behavioural problems as adults. One common result of abuse is fear aggression, in which a dog will lash out, bare his teeth, snarl and finally bite someone by whom he feels threatened. For example, your daughter may be playing with the dog one afternoon. As they play hide-and-seek, she backs the dog into a corner, and as she attempts to tease him playfully, he bites her hand. Examine the cause of this behaviour. Did your daughter ever hit the dog? Did someone who resembles your daughter hit or scream at the dog? Fortunately, fear aggression is relatively easy to correct. Have your daughter engage in only positive activities with the dog, such as feeding, petting and walking. She should not give any corrections or negative feedback. If the dog still growls or cowers away from her, allow someone else to accompany them. After approximately one week, the dog should feel that he can rely on her for many positive things, and he will also be prevented from reacting fearfully towards anyone who might resemble her.

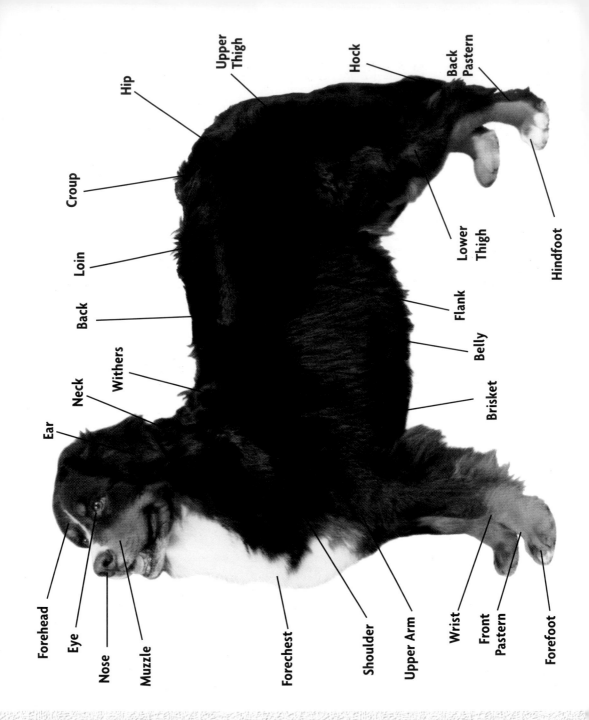

PHYSICAL STRUCTURE OF THE BERNESE MOUNTAIN DOG

Upper Thigh

Hock

Back Pastern

Hip

Croup

Lower Thigh

Hindfoot

Loin

Back

Flank

Belly

Withers

Neck

Brisket

Ear

Forehead

Eye

Nose

Muzzle

Forechest

Shoulder

Upper Arm

Wrist

Front Pastern

Forefoot

Health Care of Your

BERNESE MOUNTAIN DOG

Dogs suffer from many of the same physical illnesses as people. They might even share many of the same psychological problems. Since people usually know more about human diseases than canine maladies, many of the terms used in this chapter will be familiar but not necessarily those used by veterinary surgeons. We will use the term *x-ray*, instead of the more acceptable term *radiograph*. We will also use the familiar term *symptoms* even though dogs don't have symptoms, which are verbal descriptions of the patient's feelings; dogs have *clinical signs*. Since dogs can't speak, we have to look for clinical signs...but we still use the term *symptoms* in this book.

As a general rule, medicine is *practised*. That term is not arbitrary. Medicine is a constantly changing art as we learn more and more about genetics, electronic aids (like CAT scans) and daily laboratory advances. There are many dog maladies, like canine hip dysplasia, which are not universally treated in the same manner. Some veterinary surgeons opt for surgery more often than others do.

SELECTING A VETERINARY SURGEON

Your selection of a veterinary surgeon should not be based upon personality (as most are) but upon their convenience to your home. You want a vet who is close because you might have emergencies or need to make multiple visits for treatments. You want a vet who has services that you might require such as tattooing and grooming, as well as sophisticated pet supplies and a good reputation for ability and responsiveness. There is nothing more frustrating than having to wait a day or more to get a response from your veterinary surgeon.

All veterinary surgeons are licensed and their diplomas and/or certificates should be displayed in their waiting rooms. There are, however, many veterinary specialities that usually require further studies and internships. There are specialists in heart problems (veterinary cardiologists), skin problems (veterinary dermatologists), teeth and gum problems (veterinary dentists), eye problems (veterinary ophthalmologists) and x-rays (veterinary radiologists), as well

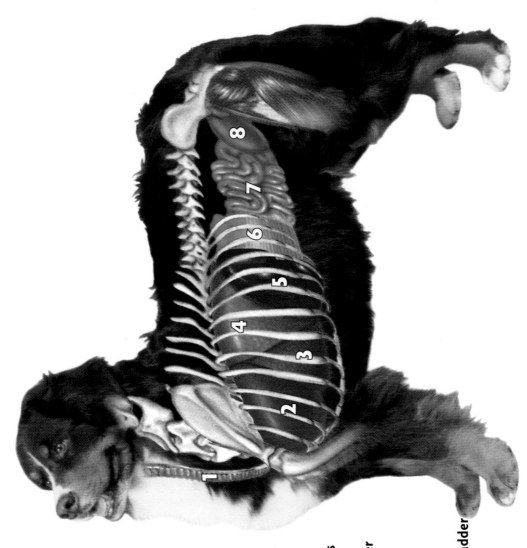

1. Oesophagus
2. Lungs
3. Gall Bladder
4. Liver
5. Kidney
6. Stomach
7. Intestines
8. Urinary Bladder

INTERNAL ORGANS OF THE BERNESE MOUNTAIN DOG

as vets who have specialities in bones, muscles or other organs. Most veterinary surgeons do routine surgery such as neutering, stitching up wounds and docking tails for those breeds in which such is required for show purposes. When the problem affecting your dog is serious, it is not unusual or impudent to get another medical opinion, although in Britain you are obliged to advise the vets concerned about this. You might also want to compare costs among

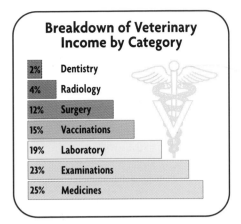

Breakdown of Veterinary Income by Category

2%	Dentistry
4%	Radiology
12%	Surgery
15%	Vaccinations
19%	Laboratory
23%	Examinations
25%	Medicines

DISEASE REFERENCE CHART

	What is it?	What causes it?	Symptoms
Leptospirosis	Severe disease that affects the internal organs; can be spread to people.	A bacterium, which is often carried by rodents, that enters through mucous membranes and spreads quickly throughout the body.	Range from fever, vomiting and loss of appetite in less severe cases to shock, irreversible kidney damage and possibly death in most severe cases.
Rabies	Potentially deadly virus that infects warm-blooded mammals. Not seen in United Kingdom.	Bite from a carrier of the virus, mainly wild animals.	1st stage: dog exhibits change in behaviour, fear. 2nd stage: dog's behaviour becomes more aggressive. 3rd stage: loss of coordination, trouble with bodily functions.
Parvovirus	Highly contagious virus, potentially deadly.	Ingestion of the virus, which is usually spread through the faeces of infected dogs.	Most common: severe diarrhoea. Also vomiting, fatigue, lack of appetite.
Kennel cough	Contagious respiratory infection.	Combination of types of bacteria and virus. Most common: *Bordetella bronchiseptica* bacteria and parainfluenza virus.	Chronic cough.
Distemper	Disease primarily affecting respiratory and nervous system.	Virus that is related to the human measles virus.	Mild symptoms such as fever, lack of appetite and mucous secretion progress to evidence of brain damage, 'hard pad.'
Hepatitis	Virus primarily affecting the liver.	Canine adenovirus type I (CAV-1). Enters system when dog breathes in particles.	Lesser symptoms include listlessness, diarrhoea, vomiting. More severe symptoms include 'blue-eye' (clumps of virus in eye).
Coronavirus	Virus resulting in digestive problems.	Virus is spread through infected dog's faeces.	Stomach upset evidenced by lack of appetite, vomiting, diarrhoea.

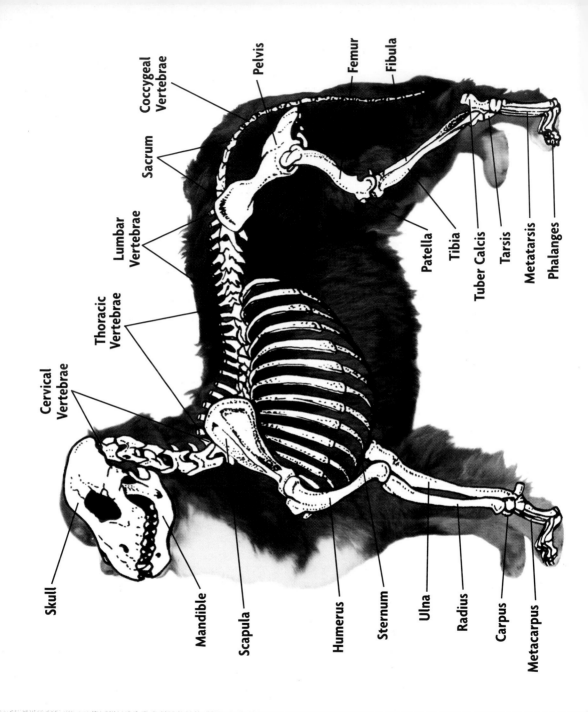

Coccygeal Vertebrae

Pelvis

Femur

Fibula

Sacrum

Patella

Tibia

Tuber Calcis

Tarsis

Metatarsis

Phalanges

Lumbar Vertebrae

Thoracic Vertebrae

Cervical Vertebrae

Skull

Mandible

Scapula

Humerus

Sternum

Ulna

Radius

Carpus

Metacarpus

SKELETAL STRUCTURE OF THE BERNESE MOUNTAIN DOG

several veterinary surgeons. Sophisticated health care and veterinary services can be very costly. It is not infrequent that important decisions are based upon financial considerations.

PREVENTATIVE MEDICINE

It is much easier, less costly and more effective to practise preventative medicine than to fight bouts of illness and disease. Properly bred puppies come from parents who were selected based upon their genetic disease profile. Their mothers should have been vaccinated, free of all internal and external parasites and properly nourished. The dam can pass on disease resistance to her puppies, which can last for eight to ten weeks. She can also pass on parasites and many infections. That's why you should visit the veterinary surgeon who cared for the dam.

PET ADVANTAGES

If you do not intend to show or breed your new puppy, your veterinary surgeon will probably recommend that you spay your female or neuter your male. Some people believe neutering leads to weight gain, but if you feed and exercise your dog properly, this is easily avoided. Spaying or neutering can actually have many positive outcomes, such as:

• training becomes easier, as the dog focuses less on the urge to mate and more on you!
• females are protected from unplanned pregnancy as well as ovarian and uterine cancers.
• males are guarded from testicular tumours and have a reduced risk of developing prostate cancer.

Talk to your vet regarding the right age to spay/neuter and other aspects of the procedure.

MORE THAN VACCINES

Vaccinations help prevent your new puppy from contracting diseases, but they do not cure them. Proper nutrition as well as parasite control keep your dog healthy and less susceptible to many dangerous diseases. Remember that your dog depends on you to ensure his well-being.

VACCINATION SCHEDULING

Most vaccinations are given by injection and should only be done by a veterinary surgeon. Both he and you should keep a record of the date of the injection, the identification of the vaccine and the amount given. Some vets give a first vaccination at eight weeks, but most dog breeders prefer the course not to commence until about ten weeks because of negating any antibodies passed on by the dam. The vaccination

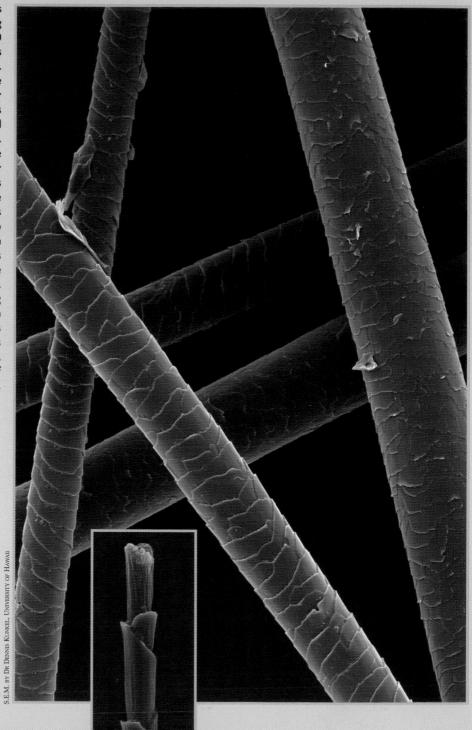

Normal hairs of a dog enlarged 200 times original size. The cuticle (outer covering) is clean and healthy. Unlike human hair that grows from the base, a dog's hair also grows from the end, as shown in the inset. Scanning electron micrographs by Dr Dennis Kunkel, University of Hawaii.

VACCINE ALLERGIES

Vaccines do not work all the time. Sometimes dogs are allergic to them and many times the antibodies, which are supposed to be stimulated by the vaccine, just are not produced. You should keep your dog in the veterinary clinic for an hour after it is vaccinated to be sure there are no allergic reactions.

scheduling is usually based on a 15-day cycle. You must take your vet's advice regarding when to vaccinate as this may differ according to the vaccine used. Most vaccinations immunize your puppy against viruses.

The usual vaccines contain immunizing doses of several different viruses such as distemper, parvovirus, parainfluenza and hepatitis although some veterinary surgeons recommend separate vaccines for each disease. There are other vaccines available when the puppy is at risk. You should rely upon professional advice. This is especially true for the booster-shot programme. Most vaccination

HEALTH AND VACCINATION SCHEDULE

Age in Weeks:	6th	8th	10th	12th	14th	16th	20-24th	1 yr
Worm Control	✔	✔	✔	✔	✔	✔	✔	
Neutering								✔
Heartworm*		✔		✔		✔	✔	
Parvovirus	✔		✔		✔		✔	✔
Distemper		✔		✔		✔		✔
Hepatitis		✔		✔		✔		✔
Leptospirosis								✔
Parainfluenza	✔		✔		✔			✔
Dental Examination		✔					✔	✔
Complete Physical		✔					✔	✔
Coronavirus				✔			✔	✔
Kennel Cough	✔							
Hip Dysplasia								✔
Rabies*							✔	

Vaccinations are not instantly effective. It takes about two weeks for the dog's immune system to develop antibodies. Most vaccinations require annual booster shots. Your veterinary surgeon should guide you in this regard.
*Not applicable in the United Kingdom

programmes require a booster when the puppy is a year old and once a year thereafter. In some cases, circumstances may require more or less frequent immunizations. Kennel cough, more formally known as tracheobronchitis, is treated with a vaccine that is sprayed into the dog's nostrils. Kennel cough is usually included in routine vaccination, but this is often not so effective as for other major diseases.

WEANING TO FIVE MONTHS OLD
Puppies should be weaned by the time they are about two months old. A puppy that remains for at least eight weeks with its mother and littermates usually adapts better to other dogs and people later in its life.

> ## KNOW WHEN TO POSTPONE A VACCINATION
> While the visit to the vet is costly, it is never advisable to update a vaccination when visiting with a sick or pregnant dog. Vaccinations should be avoided for all elderly dogs. If your dog is showing the signs of any illness or any medical condition, no matter how serious or mild, including skin irritations, do not vaccinate. Likewise, a lame dog should never be vaccinated; any dog undergoing surgery or a dog on any immunosuppressant drugs should not be vaccinated until fully recovered.

> ## VITAL SIGNS
> A dog's normal temperature is 101.5°F (38.6°C). A range of between 100°F (37°C) and 102.5°F (39°C) should be considered normal, as each dog's body sets its own temperature. It will be helpful if you take your dog's temperature when you know he is healthy and record it. Then, when you suspect that he is not feeling well, you will have a normal figure to compare the abnormal temperature against.
> The normal pulse rate for a dog is between 100 and 125 beats per minute.

Some new owners have their puppy examined by a veterinary surgeon immediately, which is a good idea. Vaccination programmes usually begin when the puppy is very young.

The puppy will have its teeth examined and have its skeletal conformation and general health checked prior to certification by the veterinary surgeon. Puppies in certain breeds have problems with their kneecaps, cataracts and other eye problems, heart murmurs and undescended testicles. They may also have personality problems and your veterinary surgeon might have training in temperament evaluation.

CUSHING'S DISEASE

Cases of hyperactive adrenal glands (Cushing's disease) have been traced to the drinking of highly chlorinated water. Aerate or age your dog's drinking water before offering it.

FIVE TO TWELVE MONTHS OF AGE

Unless you intend to breed or show your dog, neutering the puppy at six months of age is recommended. Discuss this with your veterinary surgeon. Neutering has proven to be extremely beneficial to both male and female puppies. Besides eliminating the possibility of pregnancy, it inhibits (but does not prevent) breast cancer in bitches and prostate cancer in male dogs. Under no circumstances should a bitch be spayed prior to her first season.

Your veterinary surgeon should provide your puppy with a thorough dental evaluation at six months of age, ascertaining whether all the permanent teeth have erupted properly. A home dental care regimen should be

Vitamins Recommended for Dogs

Some breeders and vets recommend the supplementation of vitamins to a dog's diet—others do not. Before embarking on a vitamin programme, consult your vet.

Vitamin / Dosage	Food source	Benefits
A / 10,000 IU/week	Eggs, butter, yoghurt, meat	Skin, eyes, hind legs, haircoat
B / Varies	Organs, cottage cheese, sardines	Appetite, fleas, heart, skin and coat
C / 2000 mg+	Fruit, legumes, leafy green vegetables	Healing, arthritis, kidneys
D / Varies	Cod liver, cheese, organs, eggs	Bones, teeth, endocrine system
E / 250 IU daily	Leafy green vegetables, meat, wheat germ oil	Skin, muscles, nerves, healing, digestion
F / Varies	Fish oils, raw meat	Heart, skin, coat, fleas
K / Varies	Naturally in body, not through food	Blood clotting

initiated at six months, including brushing weekly and providing good dental devices (such as nylon bones). Regular dental care promotes healthy teeth, fresh breath and a longer life.

ONE TO SEVEN YEARS

Once a year, your grown dog should visit the vet for an examination and vaccination boosters, if needed. Some vets recommend blood tests, thyroid level check and dental evaluation to accompany these annual visits. A thorough clinical evaluation by the vet can provide critical background information for your dog. Blood tests are often

---

A SKUNKY PROBLEM

Have you noticed your dog dragging his rump along the floor? If so, it is likely that his anal sacs are impacted or possibly infected. The anal sacs are small pouches located on both sides of the anus under the skin and muscles. They are about the size and shape of a grape and contain a foul-smelling liquid. Their contents are usually emptied when the dog has a bowel movement, but if they are not emptied completely, they will impact, which will cause your dog a lot of pain. Fortunately, your veterinary surgeon can tend to this problem easily by draining the sacs for the dog. Be aware that your dog might also empty his anal sacs in cases of extreme fright.

Don't Eat the Daisies!

Many plants and flowers are beautiful to look at, but can be highly toxic if ingested by your dog. Reactions range from abdominal pain and vomiting to convulsions and death. If the following plants are in your home, remove them. If they are outside your house or in your garden, avoid accidents by making sure your dog is never left unsupervised in those locations.

Azalea	Dumb cane	Mescal bean
Belladonna	Dutchman's breeches	Mushrooms
Bird of Paradise	Elephant's ear	Nightshade
Bulbs	Hydrangea	Philodendron
Calla lily	Jack-in-the-pulpit	Poinsettia
Cardinal flower	Jasmine	*Prunus* species
Castor bean	Jimsonweed	Tobacco
Chinaberry tree	Larkspur	Yellow jasmine
Daphne	Laurel	Yews, *Taxus* species
	Lily of the valley	

Number-One Killer Disease in Dogs: CANCER

In every age there is a word associated with a disease or plague that causes humans to shudder. In the 21st century, that word is 'cancer.' Just as cancer is the leading cause of death in humans, it claims nearly half the lives of dogs that die from a natural disease as well as half the dogs that die over the age of ten years.

Described as a genetic disease, cancer becomes a greater risk as the dog ages. Veterinary surgeons and dog owners have become increasingly aware of the threat of cancer to dogs. Statistics reveal that one dog in every five will develop cancer, the most common of which is skin cancer. Many cancers, including prostate, ovarian and breast cancer, can be avoided by spaying and neutering our dogs by the age of six months.

Early detection of cancer can save or extend your dog's life, so it is absolutely vital for owners to have their dogs examined by a qualified veterinary surgeon or oncologist immediately upon detection of any abnormality. Certain dietary guidelines have also proven to reduce the onset and spread of cancer. Foods based on fish rather than beef, due to the presence of Omega-3 fatty acids, are recommended. Other amino acids such as glutamine have significant benefits for canines, particularly those breeds that show a greater susceptibility to cancer.

Cancer management and treatments promise hope for future generations of canines. Since the disease is genetic, breeders should never breed a dog whose parents, grandparents and any related siblings have developed cancer. It is difficult to know whether to exclude an otherwise healthy dog from a breeding programme as the disease does not manifest itself until the dog's senior years.

RECOGNISE CANCER WARNING SIGNS

Since early detection can possibly rescue your dog from becoming a cancer statistic, it is essential for owners to recognise the possible signs and seek the assistance of a qualified professional.

- Abnormal bumps or lumps that continue to grow
- Bleeding or discharge from any body cavity
- Persistent stiffness or lameness
- Recurrent sores or sores that do not heal
- Inappetence
- Breathing difficulties
- Weight loss
- Bad breath or odours
- General malaise and fatigue
- Eating and swallowing problems
- Difficulty urinating and defecating

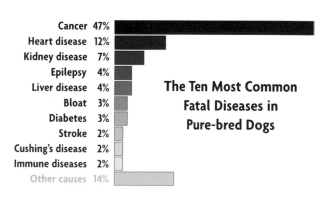

Disease	%
Cancer	47%
Heart disease	12%
Kidney disease	7%
Epilepsy	4%
Liver disease	4%
Bloat	3%
Diabetes	3%
Stroke	2%
Cushing's disease	2%
Immune diseases	2%
Other causes	14%

The Ten Most Common Fatal Diseases in Pure-bred Dogs

performed at one year of age, and dental examinations around the third or fourth birthday. In the long run, quality preventative care for your pet can save money, teeth and lives.

SKIN PROBLEMS IN BERNESE MOUNTAIN DOGS

Veterinary surgeons are consulted by dog owners for skin problems more than any other group of diseases or maladies. Dogs' skin is almost as sensitive as human skin and both suffer almost the same ailments (though the occurrence of acne in dogs is rare!). For this reason, veterinary dermatology has developed into a speciality practised by many veterinary surgeons.

Since many skin problems have visual symptoms that are almost identical, it requires the skill of an experienced veterinary dermatologist

The Eyes Have It!

Eye disease is more prevalent among dogs than most people think, ranging from slight infections that are easily treated to serious complications that can lead to permanent sight loss. Eye diseases need veterinary attention in their early stages to prevent irreparable damage. This list provides descriptions of some common eye diseases:

Cataracts: Symptoms are white or grey discoloration of the eye lens and pupil, which causes fuzzy or completely obscured vision. Surgical treatment is required to remove the damaged lens and replace it with an artificial one.

Conjunctivitis: An inflammation of the mucous membrane that lines the eye socket, leaving the eyes red and puffy with excessive discharge. This condition is easily treated with antibiotics.

Corneal damage: The cornea is the transparent covering of the iris and pupil. Injuries are difficult to detect, but manifest themselves in surface abnormality, redness, pain and discharge. Most infections of the cornea are treated with antibiotics and require immediate medical attention.

Dry eye: This condition is caused by deficient production of tears that lubricate and protect the eye surface. A telltale sign is yellow-green discharge. Left undiagnosed, your dog will experience considerable pain, infections and possibly blindness. Dry eye is commonly treated with antibiotics, although more advanced cases may require surgery.

Glaucoma: This is caused by excessive fluid pressure in the eye. Symptoms are red eyes, grey or blue discoloration, pain, enlarged eyeballs and loss of vision. Antibiotics sometimes help, but surgery may be needed.

to identify and cure many of the more severe skin disorders. Pet shops sell many treatments for skin problems, but most of the treatments are directed at symptoms and not the underlying problem(s). If your dog is suffering from a skin disorder, you should seek professional assistance as quickly as possible. As with all diseases, the earlier a problem is identified and treated, the more successful is the cure.

HEREDITARY SKIN DISORDERS
Veterinary dermatologists are currently researching a number of skin disorders that are believed to have an hereditary basis. These inherited diseases are transmitted by both parents, who appear (phenotypically) normal but have a recessive gene for the disease, meaning that they carry, but are not affected by, the disease. These diseases pose serious problems to breeders because in some instances there is no method of identifying carriers. Often the secondary diseases associated with these skin conditions are even more debilitating than the disorder itself, including cancers and respiratory problems; others can be lethal.

Among the hereditary skin disorders, for which the mode of inheritance is known, are acrodermatitis, cutaneous asthenia (Ehlers-Danlos syndrome), sebaceous adenitis, cyclic

DENTAL HEALTH
A dental examination is in order when the dog is between six months and one year of age so any permanent teeth that have erupted incorrectly can be corrected. It is important to begin a brushing routine, preferably using a two-sided brushing technique, whereby both sides of the tooth are brushed at the same time. Durable nylon and safe edible chews should be a part of your puppy's arsenal for good health, good teeth and pleasant breath. The vast majority of dogs three to four years old and older has diseases of the gums from lack of dental attention. Using the various types of dental chews can be very effective in controlling dental plaque.

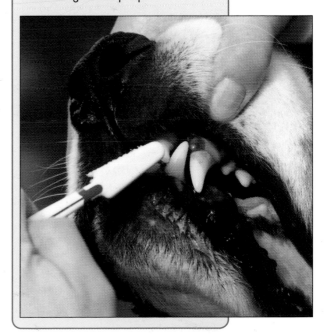

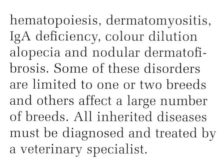

some of its damage. It may also have laid eggs to cause further problems in the near future. The itching from parasite bites is probably due to the saliva injected into the site when the parasite sucks the dog's blood.

Auto-Immune Skin Conditions

Auto-immune skin conditions are commonly referred to as being allergic to yourself, while allergies are usually inflammatory reactions to an outside stimulus. Auto-immune diseases cause serious damage to the tissues that are involved.

The best known auto-immune disease is lupus, which affects people as well as dogs. The symptoms are variable and may affect the kidneys, bones, blood chemistry and skin. It can be fatal to both dogs and humans, though it is not thought to be transmissible. It is usually successfully treated with cortisone, prednisone or a similar corticosteroid, but

hematopoiesis, dermatomyositis, IgA deficiency, colour dilution alopecia and nodular dermatofibrosis. Some of these disorders are limited to one or two breeds and others affect a large number of breeds. All inherited diseases must be diagnosed and treated by a veterinary specialist.

Parasite Bites

Many of us are allergic to insect bites. The bites itch, erupt and may even become infected. Dogs have the same reaction to fleas, ticks and/or mites. When an insect lands on you, you have the chance to whisk it away with your hand. Unfortunately, when your dog is bitten by a flea, tick or mite, it can only scratch it away or bite it. By the time the dog has been bitten, the parasite has done

extensive use of these drugs can have harmful side effects.

ACRAL LICK GRANULOMA

Many large dogs have a very poorly understood syndrome called acral lick granuloma. The manifestation of the problem is the dog's tireless attack at a specific area of the body, almost always the legs or paws. They lick so intensively that they remove the hair and skin, leaving an ugly, large wound. Tiny protuberances, which are outgrowths of new capillaries, bead on the surface of the wound. Owners who notice their dogs' biting and chewing at their extremities should have the vet determine the cause. If lick granuloma is identified, although there is no absolute cure, corticosteroids are the most common treatment.

AIRBORNE ALLERGIES

An interesting allergy is pollen allergy. Humans have hay fever, rose fever and other fevers with which they suffer during the pollinating season. Many dogs suffer the same allergies. When the pollen count is high, your dog

THE GRASS WITHERS . . .
Dogs who have been exposed to lawns sprayed with herbicides have double and triple the rate of malignant lymphoma. Town dogs are especially at risk, as they are exposed to tailored lawns and gardens. Dogs perspire and absorb through their footpads. Be careful where your dog walks and always avoid any area that appears yellowed from chemical overspray.

might suffer but don't expect him to sneeze and have a runny nose like humans. Dogs react to pollen allergies the same way they react to fleas—they scratch and bite themselves.

Dogs, like humans, can be tested for allergens. Discuss the testing with your veterinary dermatologist.

FOOD PROBLEMS

FOOD ALLERGIES

Dogs are allergic to many foods that are best-sellers and highly recommended by breeders and

THE SAME ALLERGIES
Chances are that you and your dog will have the same allergies. Your allergies are readily recognisable and usually easily treated. Your dog's allergies may be masked.

> **DID YOU KNOW?**
> Your dog's protein needs are change-able. High activity level, stress, climate and other physical factors may require your dog to have more protein in his diet. Check with your veterinary surgeon.

veterinary surgeons. Changing the brand of food that you buy may not eliminate the problem if the element to which the dog is allergic is contained in the new brand.

Recognising a food allergy is difficult. Humans vomit or have rashes when they eat a food to which they are allergic. Dogs neither vomit nor (usually) develop a rash. They react in the same manner as they do to an airborne or flea allergy; they itch, scratch and bite, thus making the diagnosis extremely difficult. While pollen allergies and parasite bites are usually seasonal, food allergies are year-round problems.

FOOD INTOLERANCE
Food intolerance is the inability of the dog to completely digest certain foods. Puppies that may have done very well on their mother's milk may not do well on cow's milk. The result of this food intolerance may be loose bowels, passing gas and stomach pains. These are the only obvious symptoms of food intolerance and that makes diagnosis difficult.

TREATING FOOD PROBLEMS
It is possible to handle food allergies and food intolerance yourself. Put your dog on a diet that it has never had. Obviously if it has never eaten this new food it can't have been allergic or intolerant of it. Start with a single ingredient that is not in the dog's diet at the present time. Ingredients like chopped beef or fish are common in dogs' diets, so try something more exotic like rabbit, pheasant or even just vegetables. Keep the dog on this diet (with no additives) for a month. If the symptoms of food allergy or intolerance disappear, chances are your dog has a food allergy.

Don't think that the single ingredient cured the problem. You still must find a suitable diet and ascertain which ingredient in the old diet was objectionable. This is most easily done by adding ingredients to the new diet one at a time. Let the dog stay on the

> **PROPER DIET**
> Feeding your dog properly is very important. An incorrect diet could affect the dog's health, behaviour and nervous system, possibly making a normal dog into an aggressive one.

modified diet for a month before you add another ingredient. Eventually, you will determine the ingredient that caused the adverse reaction.

An alternative method is to carefully study the ingredients in the diet to which your dog is allergic or intolerant. Identify the main ingredient in this diet and eliminate the main ingredient by buying a different food that does not have that ingredient. Keep experimenting until the symptoms disappear after one month on the new diet.

FAT OR FICTION?

The myth that dogs need extra fat in their diets can be harmful. Should your vet recommend extra fat, use safflower oil instead of animal oils. Safflower oil has been shown to be less likely to cause allergic reactions.

Fatty Risks

Large breeds like the Bernese Mountain dog can frequently suffer from obesity. Studies show that nearly 30 percent of our dogs are overweight, primarily from high caloric intake and low energy expenditure. The hound and gundog breeds are the most likely affected, and females are at a greater risk of obesity than males. Pet dogs that are neutered are twice as prone to obesity as intact, whole dogs.

Regardless of breed, your dog should have a visible 'waist' behind his rib cage and in front of the hind legs. There should be no fatty deposits on his hips or over his rump, and his abdomen should not be extended.

Veterinary specialists link obesity with respiratory problems, cardiac disease and liver dysfunction as well as low sperm count and abnormal oestrous cycles in breeding animals. Other complications include musculoskeletal disease (including arthritis), decreased immune competence, diabetes mellitus, hypothyroidism, pancreatitis and dermatosis. Other studies have indicated that excess fat leads to heat stress, as obese dogs cannot regulate their body temperatures as well as normal-weight dogs.

Don't be discouraged if you discover that your dog has a heart problem or a complicated neurological condition requiring special attention. It is possible to tend to his special medical needs. Veterinary specialists focus on areas such as cardiology, neurology and oncology. Veterinary medical associations require rigorous training and experience before granting certification in a speciality. Consulting a specialist may offer you greater peace of mind when seeking treatment for your dog.

EXTERNAL PARASITES

FLEAS

Of all the problems to which dogs are prone, none is more well known and frustrating than fleas. Flea infestation is relatively simple to cure but difficult to prevent. Parasites that are harboured inside the body are a bit more difficult to eradicate but they are easier to control.

To control flea infestation, you have to understand the flea's life cycle. Fleas are often thought of as a summertime problem, but centrally heated homes have changed the patterns and fleas can be found at any time of the year. The most effective method of flea control is a two-stage approach: one stage to kill the adult fleas, and the other to control the development of pre-adult fleas. Unfortunately, no single active ingredient is effective against all stages of the life cycle.

LIFE CYCLE STAGES

During its life, a flea will pass through four life stages: egg, larva, pupa and adult. The adult stage is the most visible and irritating stage of the flea life cycle, and this is why the majority of flea-control products concentrate on this stage.

A scanning electron micrograph (S. E. M.) of a dog flea, *Ctenocephalides canis*.

S. E. M. BY DR DENNIS KUNKEL, UNIVERSITY OF HAWAII

Magnified head of a dog flea, *Ctenocephalides canis*.

S. E. M. BY DR DENNIS KUNKEL, UNIVERSITY OF HAWAII

A Look at Fleas

Fleas have been around for millions of years and have adapted to changing host animals. They are able to go through a complete life cycle in less than one month or they can extend their lives to almost two years by remaining as pupae or cocoons. They do not need blood or any other food for up to 20 months.

They have been measured as being able to jump 300,000 times and can jump 150 times their length in any direction, including straight up. Those are just a few of the reasons why they are so successful in infesting a dog!

The fact is that adult fleas account for only 1% of the total flea population, and the other 99% exist in pre-adult stages, i.e. eggs, larvae and pupae. The pre-adult stages are barely visible to the naked eye.

THE LIFE CYCLE OF THE FLEA

Eggs are laid on the dog, usually in quantities of about 20 or 30, several times a day. The female adult flea must have a blood meal before each egg-laying session. When first laid, the eggs will cling to the dog's fur, as the eggs are still moist. However, they will quickly dry out and fall from the dog, especially if the dog moves around or scratches. Many eggs will fall off in the dog's favourite area or an area in which he spends a lot of time, such as his bed.

Once the eggs fall from the dog onto the carpet or furniture, they will hatch into larvae. This takes from one to ten days. Larvae are not particularly mobile, and will usually travel only a few inches from where they hatch. However, they do have a tendency to move away from light and heavy traffic—under furniture and behind doors are common places to find high quantities of flea larvae.

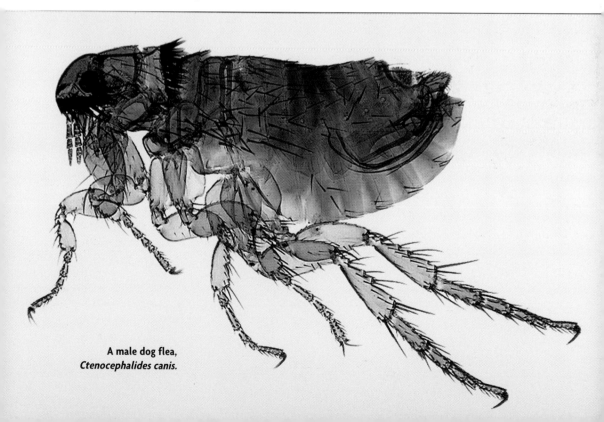

A male dog flea,
Ctenocephalides canis.

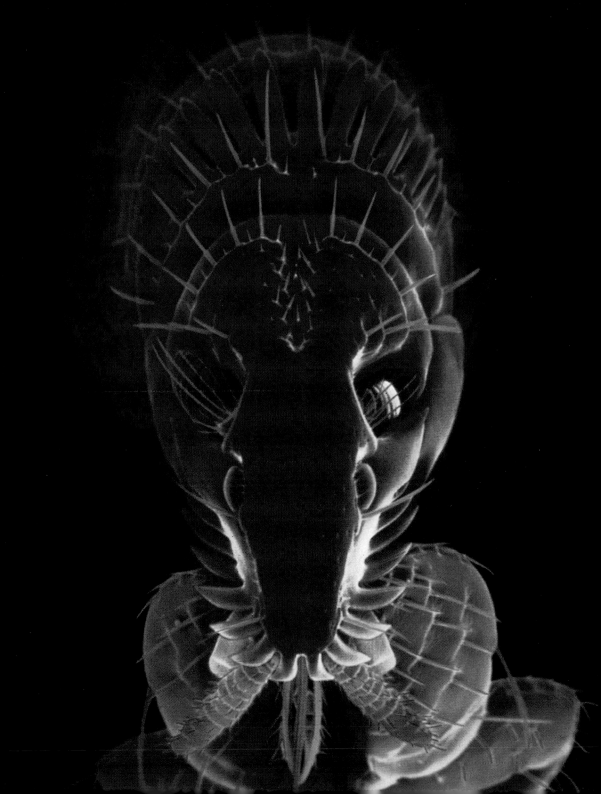

The flea larvae feed on dead organic matter, including adult flea faeces, until they are ready to change into adult fleas. Fleas will usually remain as larvae for around seven days. After this period, the larvae will pupate into protective pupae. While inside the pupae, the larvae will undergo metamorphosis and change into adult fleas. This can take as little time as a few days, but the adult fleas can remain inside the pupae waiting to hatch for up to two years. The pupae are signalled to hatch by certain stimuli, such as physical pressure—the pupae's being stepped on, heat from an animal lying on the pupae or increased carbon dioxide levels and vibrations—indicating that a suitable host is available.

Once hatched, the adult flea must feed within a few days. Once the adult flea finds a host, it will not leave voluntarily. It only becomes dislodged by grooming or the host animal's scratching. The adult flea will remain on the host for the duration of its life unless forcibly removed.

> ### DID YOU KNOW?
> Never mix flea control products without first consulting your veterinary surgeon. Some products can become toxic when combined with others and can cause serious or fatal consequences.

> ### DID YOU KNOW?
> Flea-killers are poisonous. You should not spray these toxic chemicals on areas of a dog's body that he licks, on his genitals or on his face. Flea killers taken internally are a better answer, but check with your vet in case internal therapy is not advised for your dog.

TREATING THE ENVIRONMENT AND THE DOG

Treating fleas should be a two-pronged attack. First, the environment needs to be treated; this includes carpets and furniture, especially the dog's bedding and areas underneath furniture. The environment should be treated with a household spray containing an Insect Growth Regulator (IGR) and an insecticide to kill the adult fleas. Most IGRs are effective against eggs and larvae; they actually mimic the fleas' own hormones and stop the eggs and larvae from developing into adult fleas. There are currently no treatments available to attack the pupa stage of the life cycle, so the adult insecticide is used to kill the newly hatched adult fleas before they find a host. Most IGRs are active for many months, whilst adult insecticides are only active for a few days.

When treating with a household spray, it is a good idea to vacuum before applying the

Opposite page: A scanning electron micrograph of a dog or cat flea, *Ctenocephalides*, magnified more than 100x. This image has been colorized for effect.

The Life Cycle of the Flea

Eggs

Larva

Pupa

Adult

Photos courtesy of Fleabusters® Rx for Fleas.

Flea Control

IGR (INSECT GROWTH REGULATOR)

Two types of products should be used when treating fleas—a product to treat the pet and a product to treat the home. Adult fleas represent less than 1% of the flea population. The pre-adult fleas (eggs, larvae and pupae) represent more than 99% of the flea population and are found in the environment; it is in the case of pre-adult fleas that products containing an Insect Growth Regulator (IGR) should be used in the home.

IGRs are a new class of compounds used to prevent the development of insects. They do not kill the insect outright, but instead use the insect's biology against it to stop it from completing its growth. Products that contain methoprene are the world's first and leading IGRs. Used to control fleas and other insects, this type of IGR will stop flea larvae from developing and protect the house for up to seven months.

EN GARDE:
CATCHING FLEAS OFF GUARD!

Consider the following ways to arm yourself against fleas:

• Add a small amount of pennyroyal or eucalyptus oil to your dog's bath. These natural remedies repel fleas.

• Supplement your dog's food with fresh garlic (minced or grated) and a hearty amount of brewer's yeast, both of which ward off fleas.

• Use a flea comb on your dog daily. Submerge fleas in a cup of bleach to kill them quickly.

• Confine the dog to only a few rooms to limit the spread of fleas in the home.

• Vacuum daily...and get all of the crevices! Dispose of the bag every few days until the problem is under control.

• Wash your dog's bedding daily. Cover cushions where your dog sleeps with towels, and wash the towels often.

product. This stimulates as many pupae as possible to hatch into adult fleas. The vacuum cleaner should also be treated with a flea treatment to prevent the eggs and larvae that have been hoovered into the vacuum bag from hatching.

The second stage of treatment is to apply an adult insecticide to the dog. Traditionally, this would be in the form of a collar or a spray, but more recent innovations include digestible insecticides that poison the fleas when they ingest the dog's blood. Alternatively, there are drops that, when placed on the back of the animal's neck, spread throughout the fur and skin to kill adult fleas.

PHOTO BY DWIGHT R KUHN

Dwight R Kuhn's magnificent action photo showing a flea jumping from a dog's back.

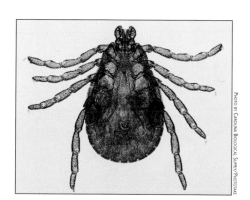

PHOTO BY CAROLINA BIOLOGICAL SUPPLY/PHOTOTAKE

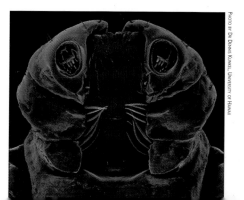

PHOTO BY DR DENNIS KUNKEL, UNIVERSITY OF HAWAII

TICKS AND MITES

Though not as common as fleas, ticks and mites are found all over the tropical and temperate world. They don't bite, like fleas; they harpoon. They dig their sharp proboscis (nose) into the dog's skin and drink the blood. Their only food and drink is dog's blood. Dogs can get Lyme disease, Rocky Mountain spotted fever (normally found in the US only), paralysis and many other diseases from ticks and mites. They may live where fleas are found and they like to hide in cracks or seams in walls wherever dogs live. They are controlled the same way fleas

A brown dog tick, *Rhipicephalus sanguineus*, is an uncommon but annoying tick found on dogs.

The head of a dog tick, *Dermacentor variabilis*, enlarged and coloured for effect.

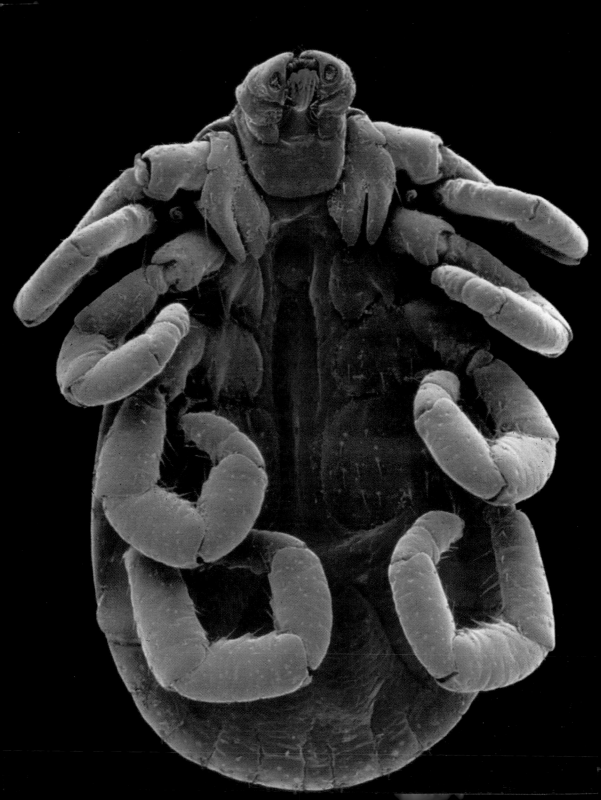

are controlled.

The dog tick, *Dermacentor variabilis*, may well be the most common dog tick in many geographical areas, especially those areas where the climate is hot and humid.

Most dog ticks have life expectancies of a week to six months, depending upon climatic conditions. They can neither jump nor fly, but they can crawl slowly and can range up to 5 metres (16 feet) to reach a sleeping or unsuspecting dog.

BEWARE THE DEER TICK

The great outdoors may be fun for your dog, but it also is a home to dangerous ticks. Deer ticks carry a bacterium known as *Borrelia burgdorferi* and are most active in the autumn and spring. When infections are caught early, penicillin and tetracycline are effective antibiotics, but if left untreated the bacteria may cause neurological, kidney and cardiac problems as well as long-term trouble with walking and painful joints.

Opposite page: The dog tick, *Dermacentor variabilis*, is probably the most common tick found on dogs. Look at the strength in its eight legs! No wonder it's hard to detach them.

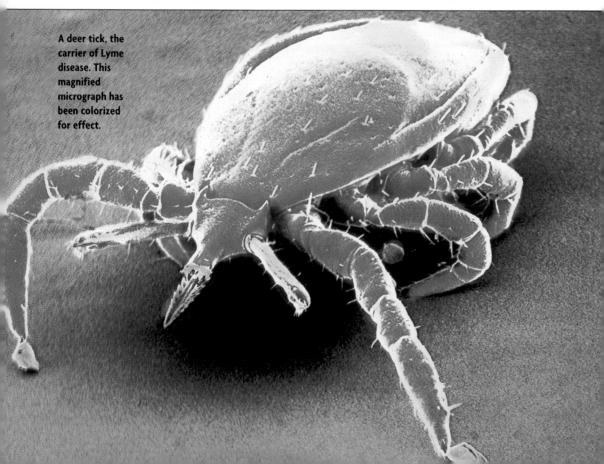

A deer tick, the carrier of Lyme disease. This magnified micrograph has been colorized for effect.

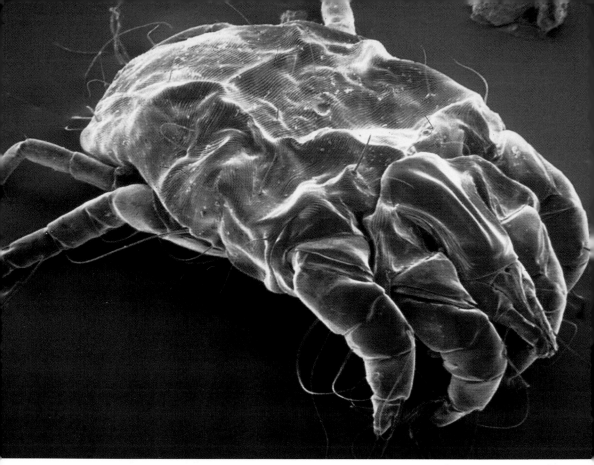

The mange mite, *Psoroptes bovis.*

PHOTO BY DWIGHT R KUHN

Human lice look like dog lice; the two are closely related.

MANGE

Mites cause a skin irritation called mange. Some are contagious, like *Cheyletiella*, ear mites, scabies and chiggers. Mites that cause ear-mite infestations are usually controlled with Lindane, which can only be administered by a vet, followed by Tresaderm at home.

It is essential that your dog be treated for mange as quickly as possible because some forms of mange are transmissible to people.

INTERNAL PARASITES

Most animals—fishes, birds and mammals, including dogs and humans—have worms and other parasites that live inside their bodies. According to Dr Herbert R Axelrod, the fish pathologist, there are two kinds of parasites: dumb and smart. The smart parasites live in peaceful cooperation with their hosts (symbiosis), while the dumb parasites kill their hosts. Most of the worm infections are relatively easy to control. If they are not controlled, they weaken the host dog to the point that other medical problems occur, but they are not dumb parasites.

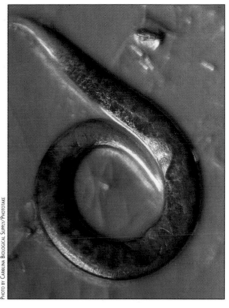

The roundworm, *Rhabditis.* The roundworm can infect both dogs and humans.

PHOTO BY CAROLINA BIOLOGICAL SUPPLY/PHOTOTAKE

ROUNDWORM

Average size dogs can pass 1,360,000 roundworm eggs every day.

For example, if there were only 1 million dogs in the world, the world would be saturated with 1,300 metric tonnes of dog faeces. These faeces would contain 15,000,000,000 roundworm eggs.

It's known that 7–31% of home gardens and children's play boxes in the US contain roundworm eggs.

Flushing dog's faeces down the toilet is not a safe practice because the usual sewage treatments do not destroy roundworm eggs.

Infected puppies start shedding roundworm eggs at 3 weeks of age. They can be infected by their mother's milk.

ROUNDWORMS

The roundworms that infect dogs are scientifically known as *Toxocara canis*. They live in the dog's intestines. The worms shed eggs continually. It has been estimated that a dog produces about 150 grammes of faeces every day. Each gramme of faeces averages 10,000–12,000 eggs of roundworms. There are no known areas in which dogs roam that do not contain roundworm eggs. The greatest danger of roundworms is that they infect people too! It is wise to have your dog tested regularly for roundworms.

Pigs also have roundworm infections that can be passed to humans and dogs. The typical roundworm parasite is called *Ascaris lumbricoides*.

DEWORMING

Ridding your puppy of worms is VERY IMPORTANT because certain worms that puppies carry, such as tapeworms and roundworms, can infect humans.

Breeders initiate a deworming programme at or about four weeks of age. The routine is repeated every two or three weeks until the puppy is three months old. The breeder from whom you obtained your puppy should provide you with the complete details of the deworming programme.

Your veterinary surgeon can prescribe and monitor the programme of deworming for you. The usual programme is treating the puppy every 15–20 days until the puppy is positively worm-free.

It is advised that you only treat your puppy with drugs that are recommended professionally.

HOOKWORMS

The worm *Ancylostoma caninum* is commonly called the dog hookworm. It is also dangerous to humans and cats. It has teeth by which it attaches itself to the intestines of the dog. It changes the site of its attachment about six times a day and the dog loses blood from each detachment, possibly causing iron-deficiency anaemia. Hookworms are easily purged from the dog with many medications. Milbemycin oxime, which also serves as a heartworm preventative in Collies, can be used for this purpose.

In Britain the 'temperate climate' hookworm (*Uncinaria stenocephala*) is rarely found in pet or show dogs, but can occur in hunting packs, racing Greyhounds and sheepdogs because the worms can be prevalent wherever dogs are exercised regularly on grassland.

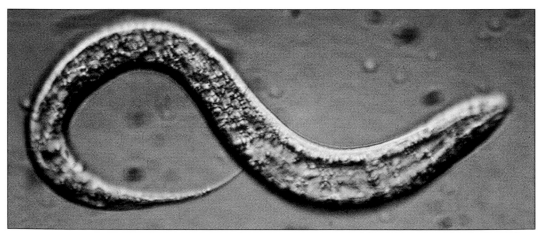

The infective stage of the hookworm larva.

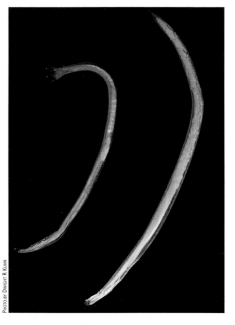

PHOTO BY DWIGHT R KUHN

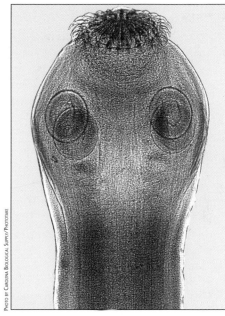

PHOTO BY CAROLINA BIOLOGICAL SUPPLY/PHOTOTAKE

Left:
Male and female hookworms, *Ancylostoma caninum*, are uncommonly found in pet or show dogs in Britain. Hookworms may infect other dogs that have exposure to grasslands.

Right:
The head and rostellum (the round prominence on the scolex) of a tapeworm, which infects dogs and humans.

TAPEWORM

Humans, rats, squirrels, foxes, coyotes, wolves, mixed breeds of dogs and purebred dogs are all susceptible to tapeworm infection. Except in humans, tapeworm is usually not a fatal infection.

Infected individuals can harbour a thousand parasitic worms.

Tapeworms have two sexes—male and female (many other worms have only one sex—male and female in the same worm).

If dogs eat infected rats or mice, they get the tapeworm disease.

One month after attaching to a dog's intestine, the worm starts shedding eggs. These eggs are infective immediately.

Infective eggs can live for a few months without a host animal.

TAPEWORMS

There are many species of tapeworm. They are carried by fleas! The dog eats the flea and starts the tapeworm cycle. Humans can also be infected with tapeworms, so don't eat fleas! Fleas are so small that your dog could pass them onto your hands, your plate or your food and thus make it possible for you to ingest a flea that is carrying tapeworm eggs.

While tapeworm infection is not life-threatening in dogs (smart parasite!), it can be the cause of a very serious liver disease for humans. About 50 percent of the humans infected with *Echinococcus multilocularis*, a type of tapeworm that causes alveolar hydatis, perish.

HEARTWORMS

Heartworms are thin, extended worms up to 30 cms (12 ins) long, which live in a dog's heart and the major blood vessels surrounding it. Dogs may have up to 200 worms. Symptoms may be loss of energy, loss of appetite, coughing, the development of a pot belly and anaemia.

Heartworms are transmitted by mosquitoes. The mosquito drinks the blood of an infected dog and takes in larvae with the blood. The larvae, called microfilaria, develop within the body of the mosquito and are passed on to the next dog bitten after the larvae mature. It takes two to three weeks for the larvae to develop to the infective stage within the body of the mosquito. Dogs should be treated at about six weeks of age, and maintained on a prophylactic dose given monthly.

Blood testing for heartworms is not necessarily indicative of how seriously your dog is infected. This is a dangerous disease. Although heartworm is a problem for dogs in America, Australia, Asia and Central Europe, dogs in the United Kingdom are not currently affected by heartworm.

The heart of a dog infected with canine heartworm, *Dirofilaria immitis*.

First Aid at a Glance

Burns
Place the affected area under cool water; use ice if only a small area is burnt.

Bee/Insect bites
Apply ice to relieve swelling; antihistamine dosed properly.

Animal bites
Clean any bleeding area; apply pressure until bleeding subsides; go to the vet.

Spider bites
Use cold compress and a pressurised pack to inhibit venom's spreading.

Antifreeze poisoning
Induce vomiting with hydrogen peroxide. Seek *immediate* veterinary help!

Fish hooks
Removal best handled by vet; hook must be cut in order to remove.

Snake bites
Pack ice around bite; contact vet quickly; identify snake for proper antivenin.

Car accident
Move dog from roadway with blanket; seek veterinary aid.

Shock
Calm the dog, keep him warm; seek immediate veterinary help.

Nosebleed
Apply cold compress to the nose; apply pressure to any visible abrasion.

Bleeding
Apply pressure above the area; treat wound by applying a cotton pack.

Heat stroke
Submerge dog in cold bath; cool down with fresh air and water; go to the vet.

Frostbite/Hypothermia
Warm the dog with a warm bath, electric blankets or hot water bottles.

Abrasions
Clean the wound and wash out thoroughly with fresh water; apply antiseptic.

 Remember: an injured dog may attempt to bite a helping hand from fear and confusion. Always muzzle the dog before trying to offer assistance.

HOMEOPATHY:
an alternative to conventional medicine

CURING OUR DOGS NATURALLY

Holistic medicine means treating the whole animal as a unique, perfect living being. Generally, holistic treatments do not suppress the symptoms that the body naturally produces, as do most medications prescribed by conventional doctors and vets. Holistic methods seek to cure disease by regaining balance and harmony in the patient's environment. Some of these methods include use of nutritional therapy, herbs, flower essences, aromatherapy, acupuncture, massage, chiropractic and, of course the most popular holistic approach, homeopathy. Homeopathy is a theory or system of treating illness with small doses of substances which, if administered in larger quantities, would produce the symptoms that the patient already has. This approach is often described as 'like cures like.' Although modern veterinary medicine is geared toward the 'quick fix,' homeopathy relies on the belief that, given the time, the body is able to heal itself and return to its natural, healthy state.

Choosing a remedy to cure a problem in our dogs is the difficult part of homeopathy. Consult with your veterinary surgeon for a professional diagnosis of your dog's symptoms. Often these symptoms require immediate conventional

'Less is Most'

Using this principle, the strength of a homeopathic remedy is measured by the number of serial dilutions that were undertaken to create it. The greater the number of serial dilutions, the greater the strength of the homeopathic remedy. The potency of a remedy that has been made by making a dilution of 1 part in 100 parts (or 1/100) is 1c or 1cH. If this remedy is subjected to a series of further dilutions, each one being 1/100, a more dilute and stronger remedy is produced. If the remedy is diluted in this way six times, it is called 6c or 6cH. A dilution of 6c is 1 part in 1,000,000,000,000. In general, higher potencies in more frequent doses are better for acute symptoms and lower potencies in more infrequent doses are more useful for chronic, long-standing problems.

care. If your vet is willing, and knowledgeable, you may attempt a homeopathic remedy. Be aware that cortisone prevents homeopathic remedies from working. There are hundreds of possibilities and combinations to cure many problems in dogs, from basic physical problems such as excessive moulting, fleas or other parasites, unattractive doggy odour, bad breath, upset tummy, dry, oily or dull coat, diarrhoea, ear problems or eye discharge (including tears and dry or mucousy matter), to behavioural abnormalities, such as fear of loud noises, habitual licking, poor appetite, excessive barking, obesity and various phobias. From alumina to zincum metallicum, the remedies span the planet and the imagination…from flowers and weeds to chemicals, insect droppings, diesel smoke and volcanic ash.

Using 'Like to Treat Like'

Unlike conventional medicines that suppress symptoms, homeopathic remedies treat illnesses with small doses of substances that, if administered in larger quantities, would produce the symptoms that the patient already has. Whilst the same homeopathic remedy can be used to treat different symptoms in different dogs, here are some interesting remedies and their uses.

Apis Mellifica
(made from honey bee venom) can be used for allergies or to reduce swelling that occurs in acutely infected kidneys.

Diesel Smoke
can be used to help control travel sickness.

Calcarea Fluorica
(made from calcium fluoride which helps harden bone structure) can be useful in treating hard lumps in tissues.

Natrum Muriaticum
(made from common salt, sodium chloride) is useful in treating thin, thirsty dogs.

Nitricum Acidum
(made from nitric acid) is used for symptoms you would expect to see from contact with acids such as lesions, especially where the skin joins the linings of body orifices or openings such as the lips and nostrils.

Symphytum
(made from the herb Knitbone, *Symphytum officianale*) is used to encourage bones to heal.

Urtica Urens
(made from the common stinging nettle) is used in treating painful, irritating rashes.

HOMEOPATHIC REMEDIES FOR YOUR DOG

Symptom/Ailment	Possible Remedy
ALLERGIES	Apis Mellifica 30c, Astacus Fluviatilis 6c, Pulsatilla 30c, Urtica Urens 6c
ALOPECIA	Alumina 30c, Lycopodium 30c, Sepia 30c, Thallium 6c
ANAL GLANDS (BLOCKED)	Hepar Sulphuris Calcareum 30c, Sanicula 6c, Silicea 6c
ARTHRITIS	Rhus Toxicodendron 6c, Bryonia Alba 6c
CATARACT	Calcarea Carbonica 6c, Conium Maculatum 6c, Phosphorus 30c, Silicea 30c
CONSTIPATION	Alumina 6c, Carbo Vegetabilis 30c, Graphites 6c, Nitricum Acidum 30c, Silicea 6c
COUGHING	Aconitum Napellus 6c, Belladonna 30c, Hyoscyamus Niger 30c, Phosphorus 30c
DIARRHOEA	Arsenicum Album 30c, Aconitum Napellus 6c, Chamomilla 30c, Mercurius Corrosivus 30c
DRY EYE	Zincum Metallicum 30c
EAR PROBLEMS	Aconitum Napellus 30c, Belladonna 30c, Hepar Sulphuris 30c, Tellurium 30c, Psorinum 200c
EYE PROBLEMS	Borax 6c, Aconitum Napellus 30c, Graphites 6c, Staphysagria 6c, Thuja Occidentalis 30c
GLAUCOMA	Aconitum Napellus 30c, Apis Mellifica 6c, Phosphorus 30c
HEAT STROKE	Belladonna 30c, Gelsemium Sempervirens 30c, Sulphur 30c
HICCOUGHS	Cinchona Deficinalis 6c
HIP DYSPLASIA	Colocynthis 6c, Rhus Toxicodendron 6c, Bryonia Alba 6c
INCONTINENCE	Argentum Nitricum 6c, Causticum 30c, Conium Maculatum 30c, Pulsatilla 30c, Sepia 30c
INSECT BITES	Apis Mellifica 30c, Cantharis 30c, Hypericum Perforatum 6c, Urtica Urens 30c
ITCHING	Alumina 30c, Arsenicum Album 30c, Carbo Vegetabilis 30c, Hypericum Perforatum 6c, Mezerium 6c, Sulphur 30c
KENNEL COUGH	Drosera 6c, Ipecacuanha 30c
MASTITIS	Apis Mellifica 30c, Belladonna 30c, Urtica Urens 1m
PATELLAR LUXATION	Gelsemium Sempervirens 6c, Rhus Toxicodendron 6c
PENIS PROBLEMS	Aconitum Napellus 30c, Hepar Sulphuris Calcareum 30c, Pulsatilla 30c, Thuja Occidentalis 6c
PUPPY TEETHING	Calcarea Carbonica 6c, Chamomilla 6c, Phytolacca 6c
TRAVEL SICKNESS	Cocculus 6c, Petroleum 6c

Recognising a Sick Dog

Unlike colicky babies and cranky children, our canine kids cannot tell us when they are feeling ill. Therefore, there are a number of signs that owners can identify to know that their dogs are not feeling well.

Take note for physical manifestations such as:

- unusual, bad odour, including bad breath
- excessive moulting
- wax in the ears, chronic ear irritation
- oily, flaky, dull haircoat
- mucous, tearing or similar discharge in the eyes
- fleas or mites
- mucous in stool, diarrhoea
- sensitivity to petting or handling
- licking at paws, scratching face, etc.

Keep an eye out for behavioural changes as well including:

- lethargy, idleness
- lack of patience or general irritability
- lack of appetite, digestive problems
- phobias (fear of people, loud noises, etc.)
- strange behaviour, suspicion, fear
- coprophagia
- more frequent barking
- whimpering, crying

Get Well Soon

You don't need a DVR or a BVMA to provide good TLC to your sick or recovering dog, but you do need to pay attention to some details that normally wouldn't bother him. The following tips will aid Fido's recovery and get him back on his paws again:

- Keep his space free of irritating smells, like heavy perfumes and air fresheners.
- Rest is the best medicine! Avoid harsh lighting that will prevent your dog from sleeping. Shade him from bright sunlight during the day and dim the lights in the evening.
- Keep the noise level down. Animals are more sensitive to sound when they are sick.
- Be attentive to any necessary temperature adjustments. A dog with a fever needs a cool room and cold liquids. A bitch that is whelping or recovering from surgery will be more comfortable in a warm room, consuming warm liquids and food.
- You wouldn't send a sick child back to school early, so don't rush your dog back into a full routine until he seems absolutely ready.

CDS: COGNITIVE DYSFUNCTION SYNDROME
'OLD DOG SYNDROME'

There are many ways for you to evaluate old-dog syndrome. Veterinary surgeons have defined CDS (cognitive dysfunction syndrome) as the gradual deterioration of cognitive abilities. These are indicated by changes in the dog's behaviour. When a dog changes its routine response, and maladies have been eliminated as the cause of these behavioural changes, then CDS is the usual diagnosis.

More than half the dogs over 8 years old suffer some form of CDS. The older the dog, the more chance it has of suffering from CDS. In humans, doctors often dismiss the CDS behavioural changes as part of 'winding down.'

There are four major signs of CDS: frequent toilet accidents inside the home, sleeps much more or much less than normal, acts confused, and fails to respond to social stimuli.

SYMPTOMS OF CDS

FREQUENT TOILET ACCIDENTS
- Urinates in the house.
- Defecates in the house.
- Doesn't signal that he wants to go out.

SLEEP PATTERNS
- Moves much more slowly.
- Sleeps more than normal during the day.
- Sleeps less during the night.

CONFUSION
- Goes outside and just stands there.
- Appears confused with a faraway look in his eyes.
- Hides more often.
- Doesn't recognise friends.
- Doesn't come when called.
- Walks around listlessly and without a destination goal.

FAILS TO RESPOND TO SOCIAL STIMULI
- Comes to people less frequently, whether called or not.
- Doesn't tolerate petting for more than a short time.
- Doesn't come to the door when you return home from work.

The term *old* is a qualitative term. For dogs, as well as their masters, old is relative. Certainly we can all distinguish between a puppy Bernese and an adult Bernese—there are the obvious physical traits, such as size, appearance and facial expressions, and personality traits. Puppies and young dogs like to play with children. Children's natural exuberance is a good match for the seemingly endless energy of young dogs. They like to run, jump, chase and retrieve. When dogs grow older and cease their interaction with children, they are often thought of as being too old to play with the kids.

On the other hand, if a Bernese is only exposed to people over 60 years of age, its life will normally be less active and it will not seem to be getting old as its activity level slows down.

If people live to be 100 years old, dogs live to be 20 years old. While this is a good rule of thumb, it is very inaccurate. When trying to compare dog years to human years, you cannot make a generalisation about all dogs. You can make the generalisation that eight years is a good lifespan for a Bernese, which is not terribly long compared to many other breeds and reminds us how precious our time with our beloved Berner truly is. Although some Berners can live to ten or better, the prevalence of cancer in the breed threatens the life of every mountain dog.

WHAT TO LOOK FOR IN SENIORS

Depending on the individual dog, his activity level and his lifestyle, a Berner can be considered a senior by the time his is five to seven years of age. The term 'senior' does not imply that the dog is geriatric and has begun to fail in mind and body. Ageing is

> **GETTING OLD**
> The bottom line is simply that a dog is getting old when YOU think it is getting old because it slows down in its general activities, including walking, running, eating, jumping and retrieving. On the other hand, certain activities increase, such as more sleeping, more barking and more repetition of habits like going to the door without being called when you put your coat on to leave or go outdoors.

SENIOR SIGNS

An old dog starts to show one or more of the following symptoms:

- The hair on its face and paws starts to turn grey. The colour breakdown usually starts around the eyes and mouth.

- Sleep patterns are deeper and longer and the old dog is harder to awaken.

- Food intake diminishes.

- Responses to calls, whistles and other signals are ignored more and more.

- Eye contacts do not evoke tail wagging (assuming they once did).

essentially a slowing process. Humans readily admit that they feel a difference in their activity level from age 20 to 30, and then from 30 to 40, etc. By treating the six- or seven-year-old dog as a senior, owners are able to implement certain therapeutic and preventative medical strategies with the help of their veterinary surgeons. A senior-care programme should include at least two veterinary visits per year, screening sessions to determine the dog's health status, as well as nutritional counselling. Veterinary surgeons determine the senior dog's health status through a blood smear for a complete blood count, serum chemistry

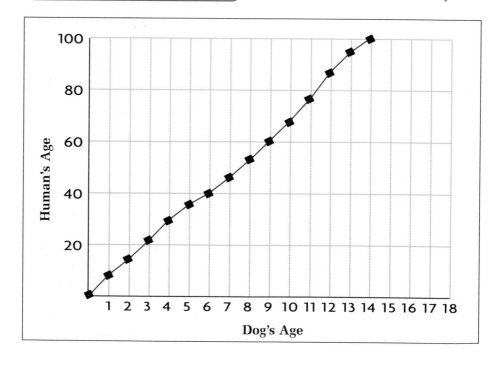

Human's Age vs Dog's Age

profile with electrolytes, urinal-
ysis, blood pressure check,
electrocardiogram, ocular
tonometry (pressure on the
eyeball) and dental prophylaxis.

Such an extensive programme
for senior dogs is well advised
before owners start to see the
obvious physical signs of ageing,
such as slower and inhibited
movement, greying, increased
sleep/nap periods and disinterest
in play and other activity. This
preventative programme promises
a longer, healthier life for the
ageing dog. Among the physical
problems common in ageing dogs
are the loss of sight and hearing,
arthritis, kidney and liver failure,
diabetes mellitus, heart disease
and Cushing's disease (a hormonal
disease).

In addition to the physical

HORMONAL PROBLEMS

Although greying is normal and
expected in older dogs, flaky or
loss of hair is not. Such coat
problems may point to a
hormonal problem, such as
hypothyroidism in which the
thyroid gland fails to produce the
normal amount of hormones.
Your veterinary surgeon can treat
hypothyroidism with an oral
supplement. The condition is
more common in certain breeds,
so discuss the likelihood with
your breeder and vet.

CONSISTENCY COUNTS

Puppies and older dogs are very
similar in their need for
consistency in their lives. Older
pets may experience hearing and
vision loss, or may just be more
easily confused by changes in
their homes. Try not to change
the feeding schedule or the diet.
Doors that are always open or
closed should remain so. Most
importantly, don't dismiss a pet
just because he's getting old;
most remain active and
important parts of their owners'
lives.

manifestations discussed, there
are some behavioural changes and
problems related to ageing dogs.
Dogs suffering from hearing or
vision loss, dental discomfort or
arthritis can become aggressive.
Likewise the near-deaf and/or

NOTICING THE SYMPTOMS

The symptoms listed below are symptoms that gradually appear and become more noticeable. They are not life threatening; however, the symptoms below are to be taken very seriously and a discussion with your veterinary surgeon is warranted:

- Your dog cries and whimpers when it moves and stops running completely.

- Convulsions start or become more serious and frequent. The usual convulsion (spasm) is when the dog stiffens and starts to tremble being unable or unwilling to move. The seizure usually lasts for 5 to 30 minutes.

- Your dog drinks more water and urinates more frequently. Wetting and bowel accidents take place indoors without warning.

- Vomiting becomes more and more frequent.

blind dog may be startled more easily and react in an unexpectedly aggressive manner. Seniors suffering from senility can become more impatient and irritable. Housesoiling accidents are associated with loss of mobility, kidney problems and loss of sphincter control as well as plaque accumulation, physiological brain changes and reactions to medications. Older dogs, just like young puppies, suffer from separation anxiety, which can lead to excessive barking, whining, housesoiling and destructive behaviour. Seniors may become fearful of everyday sounds, such as vacuum cleaners, heaters, thunder and passing traffic. Some dogs have difficulty sleeping, due to discomfort, the need for frequent toilet visits and the like.

Owners should avoid spoiling the older dog with too many fatty treats. Obesity is a common problem in older dogs and subtracts years from their lives. Keep the senior dog as trim as possible since excessive weight puts additional stress on the body's vital organs. Some breeders recommend supplementing the diet with foods high in fibre and lower in calories. Adding fresh vegetables and marrow broth to the senior's diet makes a tasty, low-calorie, low-fat supplement. Vets also offer speciality diets for senior dogs that are worth exploring.

Your dog, as he nears his twilight years, needs his owner's patience and good care more than ever. Never punish an older dog for an accident or abnormal behaviour. For all the years of love, protection and companionship that your dog has provided, he deserves special attention and courtesies. The older dog may need to relieve himself at 3 a.m. because he can no longer hold it for eight hours. Older dogs may not be able to remain crated for more than two or three hours. It may be time to give up a sofa or chair to your old friend. Although he may not seem as enthusiastic about your attention and petting, he does appreciate the considerations you offer as he gets older.

Your Berner does not understand why his world is slowing down. Owners must make the transition into the golden years as pleasant and rewarding as possible.

WHAT TO DO WHEN THE TIME COMES

You are never fully prepared to make a rational decision about putting your dog to sleep. It is very obvious that you love your Bernese Mountain Dog or you would not be reading this book. Putting a loved dog to sleep is extremely difficult. It is a decision that must be made with your veterinary surgeon. You are usually forced to make the

AN ANCIENT ACHE

As ancient a disease as any, arthritis remains poorly explained for human and dog alike. Fossils dating back 100 million years show the deterioration of arthritis. Human fossils two millions years old show the disease in man. The most common type of arthritis affecting dogs is known as osteoarthritis, which occurs in adult dogs before their senior years. Obesity aggravating the dog's joints has been cited as a factor in arthritis.

Rheumatoid disease destroys joint cartilage and causes arthritic joints. Pituitary dysfunctions as well as diabetes have been associated with arthritis. Veterinary surgeons treat arthritis variously, including aspirin, 'bed rest' in the dog's crate, physical therapy and exercise, heat therapy (with a heating pad), providing soft bedding materials, and corticosteroids (to reduce pain and swelling temporarily). Your vet will be able to recommend a course of action to help relieve your arthritic chum.

decision when one of the life-threatening symptoms listed above becomes serious enough for you to seek medical (veterinary) help.

EUTHANASIA

Euthanasia must be done by a licensed veterinary surgeon. There also may be societies for the prevention of cruelty to animals in your area. They often offer this service upon a vet's recommendation.

If the prognosis of the malady indicates the end is near and your beloved pet will only suffer more and experience no enjoyment for the balance of its life, then euthanasia is the right choice.

WHAT IS EUTHANASIA?

Euthanasia derives from the Greek meaning *good death*. In other words, it means the planned, painless killing of a dog suffering from a painful, incurable condition, or who is so aged that it cannot walk, see, eat or control its excretory functions.

Euthanasia is usually accomplished by injection with an overdose of an anaesthesia or barbiturate. Aside from the prick of the needle, the experience is usually painless.

MAKING THE DECISION

The decision to euthanise your dog is never easy. The days during which the dog becomes ill and the end occurs can be unusually stressful for you. If this is your first experience with the death of a loved one, you may need the comfort dictated by your religious beliefs. If you are the head of the family and have children, you should have involved them in the decision of putting your Bernese to sleep. Usually your dog can be maintained on drugs for a few days in order to give you ample time to make a decision. During this time, talking with members of your family or even people who have lived through this same experience can ease the burden of your inevitable decision.

THE FINAL RESTING PLACE

Dogs can have some of the same privileges as humans. The remains of your beloved dog can be buried in a pet cemetery, which is generally expensive. Dogs who have died at home can be buried in your garden in a place suitably marked with some stone or newly planted tree or bush. Alternatively, they can be cremated individually and the

Most pet cemeteries have facilities for storing your dog's ashes.

ashes returned to you. A less expensive option is mass cremation, although, of course, the ashes can not then be returned. Vets can usually arrange the cremation on your behalf. The cost of these options should always be discussed frankly and openly with your veterinary surgeon. In Britain if your dog has died at the surgery the vet legally cannot allow you to take your dog's body home.

GETTING ANOTHER DOG?

The grief of losing your beloved dog will be as lasting as the grief of losing a human friend or relative. In most cases, if your dog died of old age (if there is such a thing), it had slowed down considerably. Do you want a new Bernese puppy to replace it? Or are you better off finding a more mature Berner, say two to three years of age, which will usually be housetrained and will have an already developed personality. In this case, you can find out if you like each other after a few hours of being together.

The decision is, of course, your own. Do you want another Bernese Mountain Dog or perhaps a different breed so as to avoid comparison with your beloved friend? Most people usually buy the same breed because they know (and love) the characteristics of that breed.

Then, too, they often know people who have the same breed and perhaps they are lucky enough that one of their friends expects a litter soon. What could be better?

KEEPING SENIORS WARM
The coats of many older dogs become thinner as they age, which makes them more susceptible to cold and illness. During cold weather, limit time spent outdoors, and be extremely cautious with any artificial sources of warmth such as heat lamps, as these can cause severe burns. Your oldtimer may need a sweater to wear over his coat.

When you purchase your Bernese Mountain Dog, you will make it clear to the breeder whether you want one just as a loveable companion and pet, or if you hope to be buying an Bernese with show prospects. No reputable breeder will sell you a young puppy saying that it is *definitely* of show quality, for so much can go wrong during the early months of a puppy's development. If you plan to show, what you will hopefully have acquired is a puppy with 'show potential.'

To the novice, exhibiting a Bernese Mountain Dog in the show ring may look easy, but it takes a lot of hard work and devotion to do top winning at a show such as the prestigious Crufts Dog Show, not to mention a little luck too!

The first concept that the canine novice learns when watching a dog show is that each dog first competes against members of its own breed. Once the judge has selected the best member of each breed, provided that the show is judged on a Group system, that chosen dog will compete with other dogs in its group. Finally the best of each group will compete for Best in Show and Reserve Best in Show.

The second concept that you must understand is that the dogs are not actually comparing against one another. The judge compares each dog against the breed standard, which is a written description of the ideal specimen of the breed. While some early breed standards were indeed based on specific dogs that were famous or popular, many dedicated enthusiasts say that a perfect specimen, described in the standard, has never walked into a show ring, has never been bred and, to the woe of dog breeders around the globe, does not exist.

SEVEN GROUPS
The Kennel Club divides its dogs into seven Groups: Gundogs, Utility, Working, Toy, Terrier, Hounds and Pastoral.*

*THE PASTORAL GROUP, ESTABLISHED IN 1999, INCLUDES THOSE SHEEPDOG BREEDS PREVIOUSLY CATEGORISED IN THE WORKING GROUP.

Breeders attempt to get as close to this ideal as possible, with every litter, but theoretically the 'perfect' dog is so elusive that it is impossible. (And if the 'perfect' dog were born, breeders and judges would never agree that it was indeed 'perfect.')

If you are interested in exploring dog shows, your best bet is to join your local breed club. These clubs often host both Championship and Open Shows, and sometimes Match meetings and special events, all of which could be of interest, even if you are only an onlooker. Clubs also send out newsletters and some organise training days and seminars in order that people may learn more about their chosen breed. To locate the breed club closest to you, contact The Kennel

INFORMATION ON CLUBS
You can get information about dog shows from kennel clubs and breed clubs:

Fédération Cynologique Internationale
14, rue Leopold II, B-6530 Thuin, Belgium
www.fci.be

The Kennel Club
1-5 Clarges St., Piccadilly,
London W1Y 8AB, UK
www.the-kennel-club.org.uk

American Kennel Club
5580 Centerview Drive,
Raleigh, NC 27606-3390, USA
www.akc.org

Canadian Kennel Club
89 Skyway Ave., Suite 100,
Etobicoke, Ontario
M9W 6R4 Canada
www.ckc.ca

HOW TO ENTER A DOG SHOW
1. Obtain an entry form and show schedule from the Show Secretary.
2. Select the classes that you want to enter and complete the entry form.
3. Transfer your dog into your name at The Kennel Club. (Be sure that this matter is handled before entering.)
4. Find out how far in advance show entries must be made. Oftentimes it's more than a couple of months.

Club, the ruling body for the British dog world. The Kennel Club governs not only conformation shows but also working trials, agility trials and field trials. The Kennel Club furnishes the rules and regulations for all these events plus general dog registration and other basic requirements of dog ownership. Its annual show, called the Crufts Dog Show, held in Birmingham, is the largest benched show in England. Every year over 20,000 of the UK's best dogs qualify to participate in this marvellous show which lasts four days.

CLASSES AT DOG SHOWS

There can be as many as 18 classes per sex for your breed. Check the show schedule carefully to make sure that you have entered your dog in the appropriate class. Among the classes offered can be: Beginners; Minor Puppy (ages 6 to 9 months); Puppy (ages 6 to 12 months); Junior (ages 6 to 18 months); Beginners (handler or dog never won first place) as well as the following, each of which is defined in the schedule: Maiden; Novice; Tyro; Debutant; Undergraduate; Graduate; Post-graduate; Minor Limit; Mid Limit; Limit; Open; Veteran; Stud Dog; Brood Bitch; Progeny; Brace and Team.

The Kennel Club governs many different kinds of shows in Great Britain, Australia, South Africa and beyond. At the most competitive and prestigious of these shows, the Championship Shows, a dog can earn Challenge Certificates (CCs), and thereby become a Show Champion or a Champion. A dog must earn three Challenge Certificates under three different judges to earn the prefix of 'Sh Ch' or 'Ch.' Some breeds must also qualify in a field trial in order to gain the title of full champion. Challenge Certificates (CCs) are awarded to a very small percentage of the dogs competing, and dogs that are already Champions compete with others for these coveted CCs. The number of Challenge Certificates awarded in any one year is based upon the total number of dogs in each breed entered for competition.

There are three types of Championship Shows: an all-breed General Championship Show for all Kennel-Club-recognised breeds; a Group Championship Show that is limited to breeds within one of the groups; and a Breed Show that

SHOW RING ETIQUETTE

Just as with anything else, there is a certain etiquette to the show ring that can only be learned through experience. Showing your dog can be quite intimidating to you as a novice when it seems as if everyone else knows what they are doing. You can familiarise yourself with ring procedure beforehand by taking a class to prepare you and your dog for conformation showing or by talking with an experienced handler. When you are in the ring, listen and pay attention to the judge and follow his/her directions. Remember, even the most skilled handlers had to start somewhere. Keep it up and you too will become a proficient handler before too long!

WINNING THE TICKET

Earning a championship at Kennel Club shows is the most difficult in the world. Compared to the United States and Canada where it is relatively not 'challenging,' collecting three green tickets not only requires much time and effort, it can be very expensive! Challenge Certificates, as the tickets are properly known, are the building blocks of champions—good breeding, good handling, good training and good luck!

is usually confined to a single breed. The Kennel Club determines which breeds at which Championship Shows will have the opportunity to earn Challenge Certificates (or tickets). Serious exhibitors often will opt not to participate if the tickets are withheld at a particular show. This policy makes earning championships even more difficult to accomplish.

The Open Show is, as the name implies, open to all exhibitors and breeds. This is an excellent forum for the inexperienced owner to

Earning championships in the UK is quite difficult, and few Bernese Mountain Dogs become champions each year. This handsome exhibit seems quite on the way to a remarkable show career.

observe show protocol and gain important ring experience. There are hundreds of Open Shows each year that can be delightful social events and are great first show experiences for the novice. Even if you're considering just watching a show to wet your paws, an Open Show is a great choice.

While Championship and Open Shows are most important for the beginner to understand, there are other types of shows in which the interested dog owner can participate. Training clubs sponsor Matches that can be entered on the day of the show for a nominal fee. In these introductory-level exhibitions, two dogs are pulled out of a hat and 'matched,' the winner of that match goes on to the next round, and eventually only one dog is left undefeated.

Exemption Shows are much more light-hearted affairs with usually only four pedigree classes and several 'fun' classes, all of which can be entered on the day. Exemption Shows are

TEMPERAMENT PLUS
Although it seems that physical conformation is the only factor considered in the show ring, temperament is also of utmost importance. An aggressive or fearful dog should not be shown, as bad behaviour will not be tolerated and may pose a threat to the judge, other exhibitors, you and your dog.

sometimes held in conjunction with small agricultural shows and the proceeds must be given to a charity. Limited Shows are also available in small number, but entry is restricted to members of the club which hosts the show, although one can usually join the club when making an entry.

Before you actually step into the ring, you would be well advised to sit back and observe the judge's ring procedure. If it is your first time in the ring, do not be over-anxious and run to the front of the line. It is much better to stand back and study how the exhibitor in front of you is performing. The judge asks each handler to 'stand' the dog, hopefully showing the dog off to his best advantage. The judge will observe the dog from a distance and from different angles, approach the dog, check his teeth, overall structure, alertness and muscle tone, as

Depending on the show, your Berner could win a cup, a ribbon or a medal in conformation competition.

well as consider how well the dog 'conforms' to the standard. Most importantly, the judge will have the exhibitor move the dog around the ring in some pattern that he or she should specify (another advantage to not going first, but always listen since some judges change their directions, and the judge is always right!). Finally the judge will give the dog one last look before moving on to the next exhibitor.

If you are not in the top three at your first show, do not be discouraged. Be patient and consistent and you may eventually find yourself in the winning line-up. Remember that the winners were once in your shoes and have devoted many hours and much money to earn the placement. If you find that your dog is losing every time and never getting a nod, it may be time to consider a different dog sport or just enjoy your Bernese as a pet.

Virtually all countries with a recognised speciality breed club (sometimes called a 'parent' club) offer conformation competition specifically for and among Bernese Mountain Dogs. Under direction of the club, other special events for hunting, tracking, obedience and agility may be offered as well, whether for titling or just for fun.

SHOW QUALITY SHOWS

While you may purchase a puppy in the hope of having a successful career in the show ring, it is impossible to tell, at eight to ten weeks, whether your dog will be a contender. Some promising pups end up with minor to serious faults that prevent them from taking home a Best of Breed award, but this certainly does not mean they can't be the best of companions for you and your family. To find out if your potential show dog is show quality, enter him in a match to see how a judge evaluates him. You may also take him back to your breeder as he matures to see what he might advise.

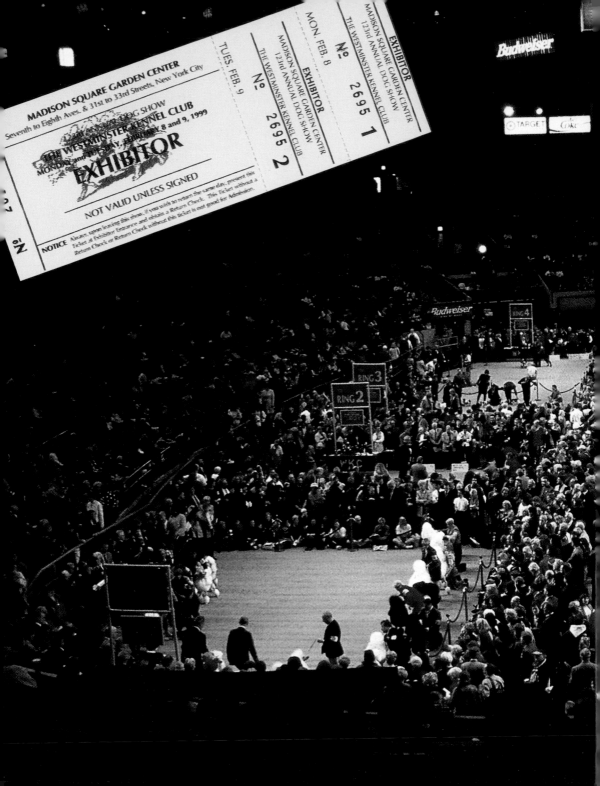

WESTMINSTER KENNEL CLUB DOG SHOW

The world's oldest dog show is the Westminster Kennel Club Dog Show, which takes place annually in New York City. The group finales are completely televised, and the show has an attendance of more than 50,000 people per day.

WORKING TRIALS

Working trials can be entered by any well-trained dog of any breed, not just Gundogs or Working dogs. Many dogs that earn the Kennel Club Good Citizen Dog award choose to participate in a working trial. There are five stakes at both open and championship levels: Companion Dog (CD), Utility Dog (UD), Working Dog (WD), Tracking Dog (TD) and Patrol Dog (PD). As in conformation shows, dogs compete against a standard and if the dog reaches the qualifying mark, it obtains a certificate. Divided into groups, each exercise must be achieved 70 percent in order for the dog to qualify. If the dog achieves 80 percent in the open level, it receives a Certificate of Merit (COM); in the championship level, it receives a Qualifying Certificate. At the CD stake, dogs must participate in four groups: Control, Stay, Agility and Search (Retrieve and Nosework). At the next three levels, UD, WD and TD, there are only three groups: Control, Agility and Nosework.

Agility consists of three jumps: a vertical scale up a six-foot wall of planks; a clear jump over a basic three-foot hurdle with a removable top bar; and a long jump across angled planks stretching nine feet.

To earn the UD, WD and TD, dogs must track approximately one-half mile for articles laid from one-half hour to three hours previously. Tracks consist of turns and legs, and fresh ground is used for each participant. The fifth stake, PD, involves teaching manwork, which is not recommended for every breed.

AGILITY TRIALS

Agility trials began in the United Kingdom in 1977 and have since spread around the world, especially to the United States, where they are very popular. The handler directs his dog over an obstacle course that includes jumps (such as those used in the working trials), as well as tyres, the dog walk, weave poles, pipe tunnels, collapsed tunnels, etc. The Kennel Club requires that dogs not be trained for agility until they are 12 months old. This dog sport is great fun for dog and owner, and interested owners should join a training club that has obstacles and experienced agility handlers who can introduce you and your dog to the 'ropes' (and tyres, tunnels, etc.).

FÉDÉRATION CYNOLOGIQUE INTERNATIONALE

Established in 1911, the Fédération Cynologique Internationale (FCI) represents the 'world kennel club.' This international body brings uniformity to the breeding, judging and showing of pure-bred dogs. Although the FCI originally included only five European nations: France, Germany, Austria, the Netherlands and Belgium (which remains its headquarters), the organisation today embraces nations on six continents and recognises well over 300 breeds of pure-bred dog. There are three titles attainable through the FCI: the International Champion, which is the most prestigious; the International Beauty Champion, which is based on aptitude certificates in different countries; and the International Trial Champion, which is based on achievement in obedience trials in different countries. Dogs from every country can participate in these impressive canine spectacles, the largest of which is the World Dog Show, hosted in a different country each year. FCI sponsors both national and international shows. The hosting country determines the judging system and breed standards are always based on the breed's country of origin.

In Switzerland the Bernese must be at least nine months of age before he can be shown, and then he may be entered only in the *Jungendklasse* (JK 9–18 months old), with dogs and bitches being shown in separate classes. The top award in an FCI show is Champion and, to gain this title, a dog must win three CACs at regional or club shows under three different judges who are breed specialists. The title of International Champion is gained by winning four CACIBs, which are offered only at international shows, with at least a one-year lapse between the first and fourth award.

The FCI is divided into ten 'Groups.' At the World Dog Show, the following 'Classes' are offered for each breed: Puppy Class (6–9 months), Youth Class (9–18 months), Open Class (15 months or older) and Champion Class. A dog can be awarded a classification of Excellent, Very Good, Good, Sufficient and Not Sufficient. Puppies can be awarded classifications of Very Promising, Promising or Not Promising. Four placements are made in each class. After all sexes and classes are judged, a Best of Breed is selected. Other special groups and classes may also be shown. Each exhibitor showing a dog receives a written evaluation from the judge.

Besides the World Dog Show and other all-breed shows, you can exhibit your dog at speciality shows held by different breed clubs. Speciality shows may have their own regulations.

INDEX

*Page numbers in **boldface** indicate illustrations.*

Acral lick granuloma 117
Adult diet 65
Age 84
Aggression
—fear 101
Agility 26
—trials 101, 154
Airlines 77
Albert Heim Foundation 12
Aldo v Tieffurt 16
Alex 17, 19
Allergies 109, 116-117
Amadeus Krauchi 19
American Kennel Club 22, 33
—address 147
American Kennel *Gazette* 22
Ancylostoma caninum 130, **131**
Ankrung 17
Appenzeller **13**, 14, 16
Arthritis 143
Ascaris lumbricoides 129
Asso v Hogerbuur 19
Auto-immune skin conditions 116
Axelrod, Dr Herbert R 129
Babette 16
Backpacking 101
Bari 11
Bathing 72
Bedding 44
Berne 10
Berner Sennenhund 14
Berner Sennenhund Klub 14
Bernese Breeders Association of Great Britain 21
Bernese Mountain Dog Club 20
—of America 22
—of Great Britain 20
Blassi 11
Boarding 77
Bones 46
Bouvier Bernois 17
Bowls 48
Breed standard 30
Breeder 57
Breeding 33
British Veterinary Association 37
Brown dog tick **125**
Burial 144
Butchers' dog 11
Canada 19

Canadian Kennel Club
—address 147
Canine development schedule 84
Canine parvovirus 116
Canis 11
Cars 76
Carting 27
Cat 92
CDS 138
Challenge Certificates 148-149
Champion 148
Championship Shows 148
Cheeseries 11
Chewing 61, 87
Cheyletiella 128
Christine v Lux 16
Christine v Schwarzwasssserbachli 16
Chweizerischer Durrbach Klub 14
Coates, Mrs Mabel 20
Cognitive Dysfunction Syndrome 138
Collar 48, **49**, 92
—choke 48
—nylon 48
—selection 49
Collis, Joyce 20
Colostrum 63
Come 96
Commands 94
Coronavirus 105
Crate 43, 45, 60, 76, 86, 88
—training 45, 88
Creigh, Mrs Irene 20
Crufts Dog Show 147
Crying 60
Ctenocephalides **123**
Ctenocephalides canis **120-121**
Cushing's disease 111
Dental health 63, 115
Dermacentor variabilis 125, **126**, 127
Destructive behaviour 142
Deworming programme 130
Diet 62
—adult 65
—grain-based 64
—puppy 63
—senior 67
Dirofilaria immitis **132**

Discipline 91
Distemper 105
Documents 38
Dog flea **125-127**
Dog tick **127**
Down 95
Draught-dog trials 27
Duntiblac Nalle 40
Durrbachler Gasthaus 11
Ear cleaning 74
Ear mite 74
—infestation 74
Echinococcus multilocularis 131
Entlebucher **13**, 14-15
Euthanasia 144
Exemption Shows 150
Exercise 69
External parasites 120-128
Farmers 11
FCI 13, 33, 154
Fear period 56
Fédération Cynologique International 13, 33, 154
—address 147
First aid 133
Flea **120-122**, 123, **124-125**
—life cycle 121, **124**
Folkdance at Forgeman 21
Fontana kennels 19
Food 62
—allergy 117
—intolerance 118
—preference 65
—problems 117
—proper diet 65
—storage 62
—treatment 118
—treats 100
Friday v Haslenbach 22
Gelbackler 11
Gender 35
Gessner, Conrad 9
Good Citizen Dog award 154
Great Britain 19
Greater Swiss Mountain Dog **13**, 14
Grooming 71-72
—equipment 72
Guard dogs 9
Guarding 25
Handling 150
Haslebacher kennel 19
Hauser, Dr 16
Heartworm **132**

Heel 98
Heim, Albert 12
Hepatitis 105
Herding 25
Hereditary diseases 35
Hereditary skin disorders 115
Hip dysplasia 17, 35-36
Histiocytosis 38
Hookworm 130, **131**
—larva **130**
House-training 83-91
— schedule 87
Hypomyelingenesis 39
Identification 79
Internal parasites 129-132
Iseli, Herr 19
Judge 150
Jungendklasse 155
Kennel Club, The 27, 30, 33, 37-38, 146-147
—address 147
—breed standard 30
Kennel cough 105, 110
Kisumu Bonne Esperance of Millwire 21
Kobe kennels 19
Kuhn, Dwight R 125
Lack Magic of Nappa 20
Leach, Mrs Egg 22
Lead 46, 92
Leptospirosis 105
Lice **128**
Life expectancy 139
Lilliman, Carol 21
Limited Shows 150
Lindane 128
Lupus 116
Magpie 20
Mange 128
—mite **128**
Matches 150
Milk 64
Mischler, Herr 16
Mite 74, 125, **128**
Mollossus 12
Mumenthaler, Gottlfried 12
Nail clipping 75
Nappa kennel 20
Neutering 111
Newfoundland 16
Nipping 59
Nutrition 66
Oasis 22
Obedience class 80, 100

Obesity 71, 142
OCD 37
Old dog syndrome 138
Osi v Allenluften 16
Osteochondritis dissecans 37
Owner considerations 29
Parasite
—external 120-128
—internal 129-132
—bites 116
Parvovirus 105
Patterson, Mrs 19
Perry, Mrs 19
Personality 24
Pluto v Erlengut 16
Pollen allergy 117
Psoroptes bovis **128**
Punishment 92
Puppy
—appearance 37
—family introduction 53
—financial responsibility 50
—first night home 54
—first trip to the vet 52
—food 63
—health 110
—home preparation 42
—ownership 40
—preparation 39
—problems 56, 59
—selection 34
—socialisation 58
—training 57-58, 81
Puppy-proofing 50, 52
Quell v Tiergarten 22
Rabies 105
Rescue dogs 26
Rhabditis **129**
Rhipicephalus sanguineus **125**
Ringgi 11
Roundworm **129**, 130
Scheidegger, Dr 12
Schertenleib, Franz 12
Schlucter, Ernst 19
Schneider, Mr Dick 20
Schweizerischer Klub 17
Seasonal Affected Disorder 64
Senior dog
—diet 67
—symptoms 142
Senior diet 67
Senta v Sumiswald 19
Separation anxiety 60, 142
Shadow, Mr 22

Show Champion 148
Showing 28
Sit 94
Skin problems 114
—acral lick granuloma 117
—allergies 117
—auto-immune 116
—inherited 115
—parasite bites 116
Socialisation 56-57, 59
St. Bernard 11-12, 16
Stalder, Fritz 19
Standard 146
Stay 95
Swiss Kennel Club 12, 17
Swiss Stud Book 12
Switzerland 9, 18
Tapeworm 130, **131**
Thorndike's Theory of Learning 91
Thorndike, Dr Edward 91
Tick **125-127**
Tickets 149
Toxocara canis 129
Toys 45-47
Tracheobronchitis 110
Training
—beginning 93
—consistency 96
—crate 88
—equipment 92
—puppy 57-58, 81
Travelling
—air 77
—car 76
Treat 57, 92
Trembler 39
Tresaderm 128
Tschanz, Frau 19
Uncinaria stenocephala 130
Vaccinations 107
Veterinary surgeon 52, 103, 118, 123, 130
Vieraugli 11
Von Nesselacker 19
Von Sumiswald kennel 19
Water 68-69
Whining 60
Working trials 26, 151
World Dog Show 155
Wurfkontrolle 17
Xodi 19

My Bernese Mountain Dog

PUT YOUR PUPPY'S FIRST PICTURE HERE

Dog's Name _____

Date _____ Photographer _____